THE UNBEARABLE BASSINGTON

SAKI was born Hector Hugh Munro in 1870 at Akyab in Burma, where his father was an officer in the British military police. His mother died two years later and Saki, together with his brother and sister, was sent to England to be raised in Devon by his grandmother and two aunts. He went to school in Exmouth and to Bedford Grammar School; later his father retired and took over his education by travelling with him widely in Europe. After a brief period in the Burma police, Saki returned once more to England where he began contributing fanciful political sketches to the *Westminster Graphic*. He wrote *The Rise of the Russian Empire* (1900) and, for six years, was a foreign correspondent for the *Morning Post* in the Balkans and Paris. His first short stories appeared in the *Westminster Gazette* and as a book, *Reginald*, in 1904. He continued to publish short stories, as well as several novels, until the outbreak of the First World War. Refusing a commission, he enlisted as a private and was killed in France in 1916.

JOAN AIKEN has written numerous books: historical, mystery, and children's novels, as well as plays and poetry. Her most recent publications include *The Smile of the Stranger*, *Arabel and Mortimer*, *The Weeping Ash*, and *The Shadow Guests*.

SAKI

The Unbearable Bassington

INTRODUCED BY
JOAN AIKEN

WITH ILLUSTRATIONS BY
OSBERT LANCASTER

Oxford   New York

OXFORD UNIVERSITY PRESS

Oxford University Press, Walton Street, Oxford OX2 6DP

London New York Toronto
Delhi Bombay Calcutta Madras Karachi
Kuala Lumpur Singapore Hong Kong Tokyo
Nairobi Dar es Salaam Cape Town
Melbourne Auckland

and associated companies in
Beirut Berlin Ibadan Mexico City Nicosia

Introduction © The Folio Society Limited 1978

This edition first published 1978 by The Folio Society Limited
First issued as an Oxford University Press paperback 1982
Reprinted 1984

British Library Cataloguing in Publication Data
Saki
The Unbearable Bassington.—(Oxford paperbacks)
I. Title
823'.912 [F] PR6025.U675
ISBN 0-19-281371-4

Printed in Great Britain by
Richard Clay (The Chaucer Press) Ltd.
Bungay, Suffolk

INTRODUCTION

BY JOAN AIKEN

SAKI'S writing is composed of four elements. Most people, asked to name their primary association with his work, would probably think of wit and absurdity; the dry fantasy of *Tobermory*, the Wildean quips of the Clovis and Reginald stories. And this wit does run through all his writing; even the saddest and most sinister stories—such as *The Hounds of Fate* or *The Wolves of Cernogratz*—contain their touches of dry humour, their sharp satirical portraits. The second element in his work is, of course, his feeling for tragedy and the supernatural, his Celtic sense of doom, which, likewise, is almost always present, even under the most light-hearted foolery: nothing ever turns out quite right in a Saki story, no plan ever succeeds, or, if it does, it rebounds and the success brings worse calamity on the perpetrator than failure would have done. Munro's childhood in Burma, his fondness for Eastern literature combined with the Celtic strain to give him a powerful sense of predestination, of fatalism. Wherever his characters go, however they act, nothing is really going to affect the ultimate outcome for them; destiny is bound to overtake them. His writing is concerned with Nemesis, rather than the culpabilities and developments of human nature.

The last two, minor but continuous, elements in his work are his active delight in town life, and his deep devotion to the country. Idyllic descriptions of London parks, clubs, theatres, Mayfair drawing-rooms, are only surpassed by nostalgic evocations of Devon lanes, farmyards, moors, and woods; the short stories are fairly equally divided between town and country settings. His novel *When William Came* shifts rhythmically in scene between London and the country, as if Munro liked to give himself a breath of country air at regular intervals—in the same way that Trollope indulged himself by inserting hunting scenes into his political novels.

Only *The Unbearable Bassington* among Saki's works is almost entirely located in London; it is essentially a town book, set within the boundaries of Mayfair and Westminster, as if the writer had deliberately planned an urban satire in order to give the most telling possible emphasis to the hero's final exile.

There is one single and significant exception to this London setting, the oddly unrelated chapter in which Elaine, the girl whom Comus loses to a more calculating rival, goes riding in the country. This in itself comes as a small shock to the reader: one even asks oneself what Elaine, a town girl, was *doing* out there in the middle of some unspecified shire, where she accidentally encounters an ex-suitor, now ill and impoverished and lodging at a farm. This scene is in contrast to the main mood of the book; instead of sharp cynicism it breathes a gentle melancholy. And it bears so little relation to the plot that the reader feels the whole incident has been introduced in order to lead up to a brief anecdote about a hurt crane in a German park, and the key sentence: '*It was lame, that was why it was tame,*' a forewarning of the book's end, the despair of being reduced by circumstances to a hideously uncongenial existence. Elaine will discover this for herself, and so, even more drastically, will Comus. The line about the crane is charged with meaning. But why did Saki elaborately set up a country background in order to deliver this message? It is as if, longing for a change of scene, he suddenly and arbitrarily abandoned his own unities.

Apart from this single odd divergence, *The Unbearable Bassington* is constructed with beautiful economy and neatness. It is a sharp, tough book; the gentler side of Munro's nature, as manifested almost entirely by his attitude to animals, a few old people and the countryside, is significantly lacking; the story's tragedy is virtually unrelieved by any touch of sympathy. Even Elaine, with her 'look of grave, reflective calm' and resemblance to a Leonardo portrait, is a malicious girl, who appears to be motivated mainly by a wish to put down and outdo her cousin.

' "As an old lady of my acquaintance observed the other day, some people are born with a sense of how to clothe themselves . . . others look as if their clothes had been thrust upon them." [Elaine] gave Lady Caroline her due quotation marks, but the sudden tactfulness with which she looked away from her cousin's frock was entirely her own idea.'

Only one minor character, Lady Veula Croot, is in the least degree sympathetic; the others are either brilliantly depicted bores—Saki shares with Jane Austen the ability to portray a bore without *being* boring—or cruel wits; the bores continuously give utterances to inanities which are instantly pounced on and held up to ridicule by the wits:

‘ "The tears in their eyes and in their voices when they thanked me, would be impossible to describe."

‘ "Thank you all the same for describing it," said Comus.’

‘ "I pointed out at some length a thing that few people ever stop to consider——"

‘Francesca went over immediately but decorously to the majority that will not stop to consider.’

The wits and the bores together make up London society, and spend their time jostling round the Mayfair scene of bridge afternoons, dinners, concerts, first nights and private views.

Comus Bassington, the main figure, was said by Saki's sister, Ethel Munro, to have been based on a real character. Even if the character was taken from life, however, it is almost certain that the plot was Munro's invention; its structure shows all the workmanlike elegance manifested in his short stories. The theme is simple: Comus's mother, Francesca, a selfish, materialistic woman, is activated entirely by the wish to maintain her occupance of her desirable London house, which is due to pass to a niece upon the niece's marriage. Can she persuade Comus, Francesca wonders, to marry the niece, and so secure the house? Or, failing that, can she manoeuvre Comus into a well-paid job, so that he can support her, or, failing that, marriage to an heiress? But relations between mother and son have deteriorated to such a pitch that Francesca has only to indicate a wish for Comus to frustrate it. He blocks her aims in three swift, irreversible moves: by casual, unnecessary cruelty to the niece's schoolboy brother, by public ridicule of the family friend who might have found him a job in the diplomatic service, and by wantonly throwing away his chances with the heiress, Elaine, who is really fond of him, but, piqued by his total lack of consideration, accepts an equally egotistical but far shrewder man, Courtenay Youghal. He, Saki assures the reader, will make her even more unhappy than Comus would have.

7

The reader may take leave to doubt this. Comus differs from Clovis, Reginald, or Bertie van Tahn, the heroes of Saki's short stories, in that his charm has to be taken on trust. Saki frequently asserts that his hero is delightful, captivating, overflowing with wit and spirits—'In many respects he was adorable; in all respects he was certainly damned'—but we never see his charm in action; on the page, Comus is *never* adorable. He is by turns cruel, petulant, tiresome, teasing, sulky, slightly dishonest, selfish, and demanding, borrowing money from Elaine, and urging his mother to sell her greatest treasure, her cherished Dutch Old Master. Comus's rival, Courtenay, is represented as a far more civilized, if not more likeable person, and though we are informed that Courtenay is shallow and will never achieve anything, there seems no reason to suppose that Comus is any better. The latter, with his complete rejection of work, spendthrift habits 'frank and undisguised indifference to other people's interests' is, ahead of his time, the complete drop-out. But this, I think, reinforces Saki's point. We are not being asked to lament the waste of a brilliant career, or a valuable life, when Comus, sacrificed at last to his mother's callous selfishness, is shipped off to a dismal job in West Africa where he will die of fever. The book's indignation is deployed in the simple perennial battle of youth against age, youth feeling itself cut off too soon. This was a recurrent theme in Saki's work.

'If you knew how I hate death! I'm not a coward, but I do so want to live. Life is so horribly fascinating when one is young, and I've tasted so little of it yet!' cries the main character in his play *The Death-Trap*. And Kurt, in *Karl-Ludwig's Window*: 'I can't die in three minutes. O God! I can't do it. It isn't the jump I shrink from now—it's the ending of everything. It's too horrible to think of. To have no more life! Isadora and the Baron and millions of stupid people will go on living, every day will bring them something new, and I shall never have one morsel of life after these three minutes.' This is the theme of *The Unbearable Bassington*.

Although Munro was reported to have been on cordial and devoted terms with his father, one cannot help suspecting that strong unacknowledged feelings of rebellion against parental authority must have manifested themselves in this novel.

Born in Burma in 1870, Hector Munro was shipped back to England at age two, after his mother's death, with the prognosis that he would not live to grow up. This view prevailed all through his childhood; no wonder life seemed so precious to him. To understand how hopeless he must have felt as a child, one has only to read *Sredni Vashtar*. Brought up by two wildly paranoid aunts and an ineffective grandmother, he had a fairly harrowing childhood, mitigated by strongly affectionate relations with his elder brother and sister, and love for animals and the Devon countryside in which they lived. Hector had brain-fever at nine and was taught by governesses until the age of fourteen because he was too delicate to go to school. In all, he had only three years' schooling. And yet, in spite of this extreme frailty, it seems to have been considered perfectly in order that Hector and his brother (whose bad eyesight rendered him unfit for the army) should return to Burma in their early twenties to take jobs in the Burma police force. One can hardly imagine a more unsuitable career for the boy who was too ill to go to school, who was interested in history, drawing, literature, the arts. His father, of course, came of an 'Army' family—and also belonged to the filicidal generation, stigmatized by Nicholas Mosley in his life of Julian Grenfell, who so lavishly and enthusiastically sent off their sons to be massacred in the trenches in World War I—where, in fact, Saki was to die. Child sacrifice was highly acceptable in the early decades of the twentieth century. Even so it seems astonishing that Colonel Munro—who, by all accounts, was an intelligent, affectionate parent—should have showed such a total lack of perception of his son's basic nature and needs as to ship him out to Burma. Plainly Hector suffered badly from homesickness; his letters, though characteristically amusing and descriptive, showed this:

'Owl and oaf thou art, not to see *Woman of No Importance* and *Second Mrs T. The* plays of the season; what would I not give to be able to see them!' 'The most welcome noise . . . is the whistle of the steamboat, especially when it brings English mail.'

Hector's unfitness for the tropical environment was soon made manifest by seven spells of fever in thirteen months, and he had to return to convalesce in England. Thereafter he took to the kind of career that really suited him—town life, literature, and journalism in London. *Bassington* was written in 1912, after he had published three collections of short stories, *Reginald*, *Reginald in Russia*, and *The Chronicles of Clovis*—all dealing with elegant, clever, amusing young men, thoroughly at home in their society.

But Comus Bassington is not charming, nor likeable, nor even particularly clever. Why? Because he was drawn from the life, and the writer's fondness for the real character blinded him to its imperfections? Conceivably so. But I believe the real reason is that Comus, emerging from the author's subconscious, is the archetypal child, stamping, sulking under punishment, in rebellion against parental tyranny. Bassington is an early book about the generation gap.

The end of the story, as always in Saki's work, is hinted at, not explicitly related, and is conveyed in three brief, telling scenes: Comus lingering in the theatre after the crowds have left, knowing that he will never set foot there again; and the shrilly hypocritical farewell party given by his mother, at which none of his own friends are present, and over which a shadow is cast by the appearance of the family ghost, a small black dog said to portend a death. The dog is seen only by Comus and the sympathetic Lady Veula. This is the sole touch of supernatural that Saki, a master of the uncanny, allows himself in the book. Elsewhere in his writing he wisely confined para-normal occurrences to short stories, perhaps feeling such things out of place in more serious work. However the ghost-dog was from real experience; Saki himself saw it in Paris when his father was dying in England; it was a Munro family haunt.

We do not follow Comus to the West African swamp where he will die of fever. Instead, as if we are entering into the sulky, exiled child's own imagination—'I'll go away and I'll die and *then* you'll be sorry!' we see the effect of his death on his mother, who realizes too late that she has loved him all along, that he is the only valuable thing in her life. And—another twist of the arm by the angry child—Francesca need not leave her house, the niece has become engaged to a man in the foreign service, and will not be able to marry for years. The niece too has been sacrificed. And—yet another twist—her son's death is announced to Francesca simultaneously with the discovery that her treasured Old Master is, in fact, only a copy.

See! the angry child cries, even your precious old picture isn't really any good!

This last touch, I feel, is one of Saki's rare lapses in technique. The end would have been more truly tragic if the picture had been real, underlining Francesca's realization that she had lost something far more valuable. Saki could not resist that final teasing twist, as if he longed to expose to the ultimate degree the worthlessness of the older generation's values, and this detail, I think, demonstrates completely that he was identifying with Comus, and raging at his useless immolation on the altar of bygone idols.

ILLUSTRATIONS

AUTHOR'S NOTE

This story has no moral.
If it points out an evil at any rate it suggests
no remedy.

CHAPTER I

FRANCESCA BASSINGTON sat in the drawing-room of her house in Blue Street, W., regaling herself and her estimable brother Henry with China tea and small cress sandwiches. The meal was of that elegant proportion which, while ministering sympathetically to the desires of the moment, is happily reminiscent of a satisfactory luncheon and blessedly expectant of an elaborate dinner to come.

In her younger days Francesca had been known as the beautiful Miss Greech; at forty, although much of the original beauty remained, she was just dear Francesca Bassington. No one would have dreamed of calling her sweet, but a good many people who scarcely knew her were punctilious about putting in the 'dear'.

Her enemies, in their honester moments, would have admitted that she was svelte and knew how to dress, but they would have agreed with her friends in asserting that she had no soul. When one's friends and enemies agree on any particular point they are usually wrong. Francesca herself, if pressed in an unguarded moment to describe her soul, would probably have described her drawing-room. Not that she would have considered that the one had stamped the impress of its character on the other, so that close scrutiny might reveal its outstanding features, and even suggest its hidden places, but because she might have dimly recognized that her drawing-room was her soul.

Francesca was one of those women towards whom Fate appears to have the best intentions and never to carry them into practice. With the advantages put at her disposal she might have been expected to command a more than average share of feminine happiness. So many of the things that make for fretfulness, disappointment and discouragement in a woman's life were removed from her path that she might well have been considered the fortunate Miss Greech, or later, lucky Francesca Bassington. And she was not of the perverse band of those who make a rock-garden of their souls by dragging into them all the stony griefs and unclaimed troubles they can find lying around them. Francesca loved the smooth ways and pleasant places of life; she liked not merely to look on the bright side of things, but to live there and stay there. And the fact that things had, at one time and another, gone badly with her and cheated her of some of her early illusions made her cling the closer to such good fortune as remained to her now that she seemed to have reached a calmer period of her life. To undiscriminating friends she appeared in the guise of a rather selfish woman, but it was merely the selfishness of one who had seen the happy and unhappy sides of life and wished to enjoy to the utmost what was left to her of the former. The vicissitudes of fortune had not soured her, but they had perhaps narrowed her in the sense of making her concentrate much of her sympathies on things that immediately pleased and amused her, or that recalled and perpetuated the pleasing and successful incidents of other days. And it was her drawing-room in particular that enshrined the memorials or tokens of past and present happiness.

Into that comfortable quaint-shaped room of angles and bays and alcoves had sailed, as into a harbour, those precious personal possessions and trophies that had survived the buffetings and storms of a not very tranquil married life. Wherever her eyes might turn she saw the embodied results of her successes, economies, good luck, good management or good taste. The battle had more than once gone against her, but she had somehow always contrived to save her baggage train, and her complacent gaze could roam over object after object that represented the spoils of victory or the salvage of honourable defeat. The delicious bronze Fremiet on the mantelpiece had been the outcome of a Grand Prix sweepstake of many years ago; a group of Dresden figures of some considerable value had been bequeathed to her by a discreet admirer, who had added death to his other kindnesses; another group had been a self-bestowed present, purchased in blessed and unfading memory of a wonderful nine-days' bridge winnings at a country-house party. There were old Persian and Bokharan rugs and Worcester tea-services of glowing colour, and little treasures of antique silver that each enshrined a history or a memory in addition to its own intrinsic value. It amused her at times to think of the bygone craftsmen and artificers who had hammered and wrought and woven in far distant countries and ages, to produce the wonderful and beautiful things that had come, one way and another, into her possession. Workers in the studios of medieval Italian towns and of later Paris, in the bazaars of Bagdad and of Central Asia, in old-time English workshops and German factories, in all manner of queer hidden corners where craft secrets were jealously guarded, nameless unremembered men and men whose names were world-renowned and deathless.

And above all her other treasures, dominating in her estimation every other object that the room contained, was the great Van der Meulen that had come from her father's home as part of her wedding dowry. It fitted exactly into the central wall panel above the narrow buhl cabinet, and filled exactly its right space in the composition and balance of the room. From wherever you sat it seemed to confront you as the dominating feature of its surroundings. There was a pleasing serenity about the great pompous battle scene with its solemn courtly warriors bestriding their heavily prancing steeds, grey or skewbald or dun, all gravely in earnest, and yet somehow conveying the impression that their campaigns were but vast serious picnics arranged in the grand manner. Francesca could not imagine the drawing-room without the crowning complement of the stately well-hung picture, just as she could not imagine herself in any other setting than this house in Blue Street with its crowded Pantheon of cherished household gods.

And herein sprouted one of the thorns that obtruded through the rose-leaf damask of what might otherwise have been Francesca's peace of mind. One's happiness always lies in the future rather than in the past. With due deference to an esteemed lyrical authority one may safely say that a sorrow's crown of sorrow is anticipating unhappier things. The house in Blue Street had been left to her by her old friend Sophie Chetrof, but only until such time as her niece Emmeline Chetrof should marry, when it was to pass to her as a wedding present. Emmeline was now seventeen and passably good-looking, and four or five years were all that could be safely allotted to the span of her continued spinsterhood. Beyond that period lay chaos, the wrenching asunder of Francesca from the sheltering habitation that had grown to be her soul. It is true that in imagination she had built herself a bridge across the

17

chasm, a bridge of a single span. The bridge in question was her schoolboy son Comus, now being educated somewhere in the southern counties, or rather one should say the bridge consisted of the possibility of his eventual marriage with Emmeline, in which case Francesca saw herself still reigning, a trifle squeezed and incommoded perhaps, but still reigning in the the house in Blue Street. The Van der Meulen would still catch its requisite after-noon light in its place of honour, the Fremiet and the Dresden and Old Worcester would continue undisturbed in their accustomed niches. Emmeline could have the Japanese snuggery, where Francesca sometimes drank her after-dinner coffee, as a separate drawing-room, where she could put her own things. The details of the bridge structure had all been carefully thought out. Only— it was an unfortunate circumstance that Comus should have been the span on which everything balanced.

Francesca's husband had insisted on giving the boy that strange Pagan name, and had not lived long enough to judge as to the appropriateness, or otherwise, of its significance. In seventeen years and some odd months Francesca had had ample opportunity for forming an opinion concerning her son's characteristics. The spirit of mirthfulness which one associates with the name certainly ran riot in the boy, but it was a twisted wayward sort of mirth of which Francesca herself could seldom see the humorous side. In her brother Henry, who sat eating small cress sandwiches as solemnly as though they had been ordained in some immemorial Book of Observances, fate had been undisguisedly kind to her. He might so easily have married some pretty helpless little woman, and lived at Notting Hill Gate, and been the father of a long string of pale, clever, useless children, who would have had birthdays and the sort of illnesses that one is expected to send grapes to, and who would have painted fatuous objects in a South Kensington manner as Christmas offerings to an aunt whose cubic space for lumber was limited. Instead of committing these unbrotherly actions, which are so frequent in family life that they might almost be called brotherly, Henry had married a woman who had both money and a sense of repose, and their one child had the brilliant virtue of never saying anything which even its parents could consider worth repeating. Then he had gone into Parliament, possibly with the idea of making his home life seem less dull; at any rate it redeemed his career from insignificance, for no man whose death can produce the item 'another by-election' on the news posters can be wholly a nonentity. Henry, in short, who might have been an embarrassment and a handicap, had chosen rather to be a friend and counsellor, at times even an emergency bank balance; Francesca on her part, with partiality which a clever and lazily-inclined woman often feels for a reliable fool, not only sought his counsel but frequently followed it. When convenient, moreover, she repaid his loans.

Against this good service on the part of Fate in providing her with Henry for a brother, Francesca could well set the plaguy malice of the destiny that had given her Comus for a son. The boy was one of those untameable young lords of misrule that frolic and chafe themselves through nursery and preparatory and public-school days with the utmost allowance of storm and dust and dislocation and the least possible amount of collar-work, and come somehow with a laugh through a series of catastrophes that has reduced everyone else concerned to tears or Cassandra-like forebodings. Sometimes they sober down in after-life and become uninteresting, forgetting that they were ever lords of anything; sometimes Fate plays royally into their hands, and they do great things in a spacious manner, and are thanked by Parliament and the Press and acclaimed by gala-day crowds. But in most cases their tragedy begins when they leave school and turn themselves loose in a world that has grown too civilized and too crowded and too empty to have any place for them. And they are very many.

Henry Greech had made an end of biting small sandwiches, and settled down like a dust-storm refreshed, to discuss one of the fashionably prevalent topics of the moment, the prevention of destitution.

'It is a question that is only being nibbled at, smelt at, one might say, at the present moment,' he observed, 'but it is one that will have to engage our serious attention and consideration before long. The first thing that we shall have to do is to get out of the dilettante and academic way of approaching it. We must collect and assimilate hard facts. It is a subject that ought to appeal to all thinking minds, and yet, you know, I find it surprisingly difficult to interest people in it.'

Francesca made some monosyllabic response, a sort of sympathetic grunt which was meant to indicate that she was, to a certain extent, listening and appreciating. In reality she was reflecting that Henry possibly found it difficult to interest people in any topic that he enlarged on. His talents lay so thoroughly in the direction of being uninteresting, that even as an eye-witness of the massacre of St Bartholomew he would probably have infused a flavour of boredom into his descriptions of the event.

'I was speaking down in Leicestershire the other day on this subject,' continued Henry, 'and I pointed out at some length a thing that few people ever stop to consider——'

Francesca went over immediately but decorously to the majority that will not stop to consider.

'Did you come across any of the Barnets when you were down there?' she interrupted; 'Eliza Barnet is rather taken up with all those subjects.'

In the propagandist movements of Sociology, as in other arenas of life and struggle, the fiercest competition and rivalry is frequently to be found between closely allied types and species. Eliza Barnet shared many of Henry Greech's political and social views, but she also shared his fondness for pointing things out at some length; there had been occasions when she had extensively occupied the strictly limited span allotted to the platform oratory of a group of speakers of whom Henry Greech had been an impatient unit. He might see eye to eye with her on the leading questions of the day, but he persistently wore mental blinkers as far as her estimable qualities were concerned, and the mention of her name was a skilful lure drawn across the trail of his discourse; if Francesca had to listen to his eloquence on any subject she much preferred that it should be a disparagement of Eliza Barnet rather than the prevention of destitution.

'I've no doubt she means well,' said Henry, 'but it would be a good thing if she could be induced to keep her own personality a little more in the background, and not to imagine that she is the necessary mouthpiece of all the progressive thought in the countryside. I fancy Canon Besomley must have had her in his mind when he said that some people came into the world to shake empires and others to move amendments.'

Francesca laughed with genuine amusement.

'I suppose she is really wonderfully well up in all the subjects she talks about,' was her provocative comment.

Henry grew possibly conscious of the fact that he was being drawn out on the subject of Eliza Barnet, and he presently turned on to a more personal topic.

'From the general air of tranquillity about the house I presume Comus has gone back to Thaleby,' he observed.

'Yes,' said Francesca, 'he went back yesterday. Of course, I'm very fond of him, but I bear the separation well. When he's here it's rather like having a live volcano in the house, a volcano that in its quietest moments asks incessant questions and uses strong scent.'

'It is only a temporary respite,' said Henry; 'in a year or two he will be leaving school, and then what?'

Francesca closed her eyes with the air of one who seeks to shut out a distressing vision. She was not fond of looking intimately at the future in the presence of another person, especially when the future was draped in doubtfully auspicious colours.

'And then what?' persisted Henry.

'Then I suppose he will be upon my hands.'

'Exactly.'

'Don't sit there looking judicial. I'm quite ready to listen to suggestions if you've any to make.'

'In the case of any ordinary boy,' said Henry, 'I might make lots of suggestions as to the finding of suitable employment. From what we know of Comus it would be rather a waste of time for either of us to look for jobs which he wouldn't look at when we'd got them for him.'

'He must do something,' said Francesca.

'I know he must; but he never will. At least, he'll never stick to anything. The most hopeful thing to do with him will be to marry him to an heiress. That would solve the financial side of his problem. If he had unlimited money at his disposal, he might go into the wilds somewhere and shoot big game. I never know what the big game have done to deserve it, but they do help to deflect the destructive energies of some of our social misfits.'

Henry, who never killed anything larger or fiercer than a trout, was scornfully superior on the subject of big game shooting.

Francesca brightened at the matrimonial suggestion. 'I don't know about an heiress,' she said reflectively. 'There's Emmeline Chetrof, of course. One could hardly call her an heiress, but she's got a comfortable little income of her own, and I suppose something more will come to her from her grandmother. Then, of course, you know this house goes to her when she marries.'

'That would be very convenient,' said Henry, probably following a line of thought that his sister had trodden many hundreds of times before him. 'Do she and Comus hit it off at all well together?'

'Oh, well enough in boy and girl fashion,' said Francesca. 'I must arrange for them to see more of each other in future. By the way, that little brother of hers that she dotes on, Lancelot, goes to Thaleby this term. I'll write and tell Comus to be specially kind to him; that will be a sure way to Emmeline's heart. Comus has been made a prefect, you know. Heaven knows why.'

'It can only be for prominence in games,' sniffed Henry; 'I think we may safely leave work and conduct out of the question.'

Comus was not a favourite with his uncle.

Francesca had turned to her writing cabinet and was scribbling a letter to her son in which the delicate health, timid disposition and other inevitable attributes of the new boy were brought to his notice, and commended to his care. When she had sealed and stamped the envelope Henry uttered a belated caution.

'Perhaps on the whole it would be wiser to say nothing about the boy to Comus. He doesn't always respond to directions, you know.'

Francesca did know, and already was more than half of her brother's opinion; but the woman who can sacrifice a clean unspoiled penny stamp is probably yet unborn.

CHAPTER II

LANCELOT CHETROF stood at the end of a long bare passage, restlessly consulting his watch and fervently wishing himself half an hour older with a certain painful experience already registered in the past; unfortunately it still belonged to the future, and what was still more horrible, to the immediate future. Like many boys new to a school he had cultivated an unhealthy passion for obeying rules and requirements, and his zeal in this direction had proved his undoing. In his hurry to be doing two or three estimable things at once he had omitted to study the notice-board in more than a perfunctory fashion and had thereby missed a football practice specially ordained for newly-joined boys. His fellow-juniors of a term's longer standing had graphically enlightened him as to the inevitable consequences of his lapse; the dread which attaches to the unknown was, at any rate, deleted from his approaching doom, though at the moment he felt scarcely grateful for the knowledge placed at his disposal with such lavish solicitude.

'You'll get six of the very best, over the back of a chair,' said one.

'They'll draw a chalk line across you, of course, you know,' said another.

'A chalk line?'

'Rather. So that every cut can be aimed exactly at the same spot. It hurts much more that way.'

Lancelot tried to nourish a wan hope that there might be an element of exaggeration in this uncomfortably realistic description.

Meanwhile in the prefects' room at the other end of the passage, Comus Bassington and a fellow-prefect sat also waiting on time, but in a mood of far more pleasurable expectancy. Comus was one of the most junior of the prefect caste, but by no means the least well known, and outside the masters' common-room he enjoyed a certain fitful popularity, or at any rate admiration. At football he was too erratic to be a really brilliant player, but he tackled as if the act of bringing his man headlong to the ground was in itself a sensuous pleasure, and his weird swear-words whenever he got hurt were eagerly treasured by those who were fortunate enough to hear them. At athletics in general he was a showy performer, and although new to the functions of a prefect he had already established a reputation as an effective and artistic caner. In appearance he exactly fitted his fanciful Pagan name. His large green-grey eyes seemed for ever asparkle with goblin mischief and the joy of revelry, and the curved lips might have been those of some wickedly-laughing faun; one almost expected to see embryo horns fretting the smoothness of his sleek dark hair. The chin was firm, but one looked in vain for a redeeming touch of ill-temper in the handsome, half-mocking, half-petulant face. With a strain of sourness in him Comus might have been leavened into something creative and masterful; fate had fashioned him with a certain whimsical charm, and left him all unequipped for the greater purposes of life. Perhaps no one would have called him a lovable character, but in many respects he was adorable; in all respects he was certainly damned.

Rutley, his companion of the moment, sat watching him and wondering, from the depths of a very ordinary brain, whether he liked or hated him; it was easy to do either.

'It's not really your turn to cane,' he said.

'I know it's not,' said Comus, fingering a very serviceable-looking cane as lovingly as a pious violinist might handle his Strad. 'I gave Greyson some mint-chocolate to let me toss whether I caned or him, and I won. He was rather decent over it and let me have half the chocolate back.'

The droll lightheartedness which won Comus Bassington such measure of popularity as he enjoyed among his fellows did not materially help to endear him to the succession of masters with whom he came in contact during the course of his schooldays. He amused and interested such of them as had the saving grace of humour at their disposal, but if they sighed when he passed from their immediate responsibility it was a sigh of relief rather than of regret. The more enlightened and experienced of them realized that he was something outside the scope of the things that they were called upon to deal with. A man who has been trained to cope with storms, to foresee their coming, and to minimize their con-

24

sequences, may be pardoned if he feels a certain reluctance to measure himself against a tornado.

Men of more limited outlook and with a correspondingly larger belief in their own powers were ready to tackle the tornado had time permitted.

'I think I could tame young Bassington if I had your opportunities,' a form-master once remarked to a colleague whose House had the embarrassing distinction of numbering Comus among its inmates.

'Heaven forbid that I should try,' replied the housemaster.

'But why?' asked the reformer.

'Because Nature hates any interference with her own arrangements, and if you start in to tame the obviously untameable you are taking a fearful responsibility on yourself.'

'Nonsense; boys are Nature's raw material.'

'Millions of boys are. There are just a few, and Bassington is one of them, who are Nature's highly finished product when they are in the schoolboy stage, and we, who are supposed to be moulding raw material, are quite helpless when we come in contact with them.'

'But what happens to them when they grow up?'

'They never do grow up,' said the housemaster; 'that is their tragedy. Bassington will certainly never grow out of his present stage.'

'Now you are talking in the language of Peter Pan,' said the form-master.

'I am not thinking in the manner of Peter Pan,' said the other. 'With all reverence for the author of that masterpiece I should say he had a wonderful and tender insight into the child mind and knew nothing whatever about boys. To make only one criticism on that particular work, can you imagine a lot of British boys, or boys of any country that one knows of, who would stay contentedly playing children's games in an underground cave when there were wolves and pirates and Red Indians to be had for the asking on the other side of the trap door?'

The form-master laughed. 'You evidently think that the "Boy who would not grow up" must have been written by a "grown-up who could never have been a boy". Perhaps that is the meaning of the "Never-never Land". I daresay you're right in your criticism, but I don't agree with you about Bassington. He's a handful to deal with, as anyone knows who has come in contact with him, but if one's hands weren't full with a thousand and one other things I hold to my opinion that he could be tamed.'

And he went his way, having maintained a form-master's inalienable privilege of being in the right.

*

In the prefects' room, Comus busied himself with the exact position of a chair planted out in the middle of the floor.

'I think everything's ready,' he said.

Rutley glanced at the clock with the air of a Roman elegant in the Circus, languidly awaiting the introduction of an expected Christian to an expectant tiger.

'The kid is due in two minutes,' he said.

'He'd jolly well better not be late,' said Comus.

Comus had gone through the mill of many scorching castigations in his earlier schooldays, and was able to appreciate to the last ounce the panic that must be now possessing his foredoomed victim, probably at this moment hovering miserably outside the door. After all, that was part of the fun of the thing, and most things have their amusing side if one knows where to look for it.

There was a knock at the door, and Lancelot entered in response to a hearty friendly summons to 'come in'.

'I've come to be caned,' he said breathlessly; adding by way of identification, 'my name's Chetrof.'

'That's quite bad enough in itself,' said Comus, 'but there is probably worse to follow. You are evidently keeping something back from us.'

'I missed a footer practice,' said Lancelot.

'Six,' said Comus briefly, picking up his cane.

'I didn't see the notice on the board,' hazarded Lancelot as a forlorn hope.

'We are always pleased to listen to excuses, and our charge is two extra cuts. That will be eight. Get over.'

And Comus indicated the chair that stood in sinister isolation in the middle of the room. Never had an article of furniture seemed more hateful in Lancelot's eyes. Comus could well remember the

time when a chair stuck in the middle of a room had seemed to him the most horrible of manufactured things.

'Lend me a piece of chalk,' he said to his brother prefect.

Lancelot ruefully recognized the truth of the chalk-line story.

Comus drew the desired line with an anxious exactitude which he would have scorned to apply to a diagram of Euclid or a map of the Russo-Persian frontier.

'Bend a little more forward,' he said to the victim, 'and much tighter. Don't trouble to look pleasant, because I can't see your face anyway. It may sound unorthodox to say so, but this is going to hurt you much more than it will hurt me.'

There was a carefully measured pause, and then Lancelot was made vividly aware of what a good cane can be made to do in really efficient hands. At the second cut he projected himself hurriedly off the chair.

'Now I've lost count,' said Comus; 'we shall have to begin all over again. Kindly get back into the same position. If you get down again before I've finished Rutley will hold you over and you'll get a dozen.'

Lancelot got back on to the chair, and was re-arranged to the taste of his executioner. He stayed there somehow or other while Comus made eight accurate and agonizingly effective shots at the chalk line.

'By the way,' he said to his gasping and gulping victim when the infliction was over, 'you said Chetrof, didn't you? I believe I've been asked to be kind to you. As a beginning you can clean out my study this afternoon. Be awfully careful how you dust the old china. If you break any don't come and tell me, but just go and drown yourself somewhere; it will save you from a worse fate.'

'I don't know where your study is,' said Lancelot between his chokes.

'You'd better find it or I shall have to beat you, really hard this time. Here, you'd better keep this chalk in your pocket, it's sure to come in handy later on. Don't stop to thank me for all I've done, it only embarrasses me.'

As Comus hadn't got a study Lancelot spent a feverish half-hour in looking for it, incidentally missing another footer practice.

*

'Everything is very jolly here,' wrote Lancelot to his sister Emmeline. 'The prefects can give you an awful hot time if they like, but most of them are rather decent. Some are Beasts. Bassington is a prefect, though only a junior one. He is the Limit as Beasts go. At least, I think so.'

Schoolboy reticence went no further, but Emmeline filled in the gaps for herself with the lavish splendour of feminine imagination. Francesca's bridge went crashing into the abyss.

CHAPTER III

O N the evening of a certain November day, two years after the events heretofore chronicled, Francesca Bassington steered her way through the crowd that filled the rooms of her friend Serena Golackly, bestowing nods of vague recognition as she went, but with eyes that were obviously intent on focusing one particular figure. Parliament had pulled its energies together for an Autumn Session, and both political parties were fairly well represented in the throng. Serena had a harmless way of inviting a number of more or less public men and women to her house, and hoping that if you left them together long enough they would constitute a *salon*. In pursuance of the same instinct she planted the flower borders at her week-end cottage retreat in Surrey with a large mixture of bulbs, and called the result a Dutch garden. Unfortunately, though you may bring brilliant talkers into your home, you cannot always make them talk brilliantly, or even talk at all; what is worse you cannot restrict the output of those starling-voiced dullards who seem to have, on all subjects, so much to say that was well worth leaving unsaid. One group that Francesca passed was discussing a Spanish painter, who was forty-three, and had painted thousands of square yards of canvas in his time, but of whom no one in London had heard till a few months ago; now the starling-voices seemed determined that one should hear of very little else. Three women knew how his name was pronounced, another always felt that she must go into a forest and pray whenever she saw his pictures, another had noticed that there were always pomegranates in his later compositions, and a man with an indefensible collar knew what the pomegranates 'meant'. 'What I think so splendid about him,' said a stout lady in a loud challenging voice, 'is the way he defies all the conventions of art while retaining all that the conventions stand for.' 'Ah, but have you noticed——' put in the man with the atrocious collar, and Francesca pushed desperately on, wondering dimly as she went what people found so unsupportable in the affliction of deafness.

Her progress was impeded for a moment by a couple engaged in earnest and voluble discussion of some smouldering question of the day; a thin spectacled young man with the receding forehead that so often denotes advanced opinions, was talking to a spectacled young woman with a similar type of forehead, and exceedingly untidy hair. It was her ambition in life to be taken for a Russian girl-student, and she had spent weeks of patient research in trying to find out exactly where you put the tea-leaves in a samovar. She had once been introduced to a young Jewess from Odessa, who had died of pneumonia the following week; the experience, slight as it was, constituted the spectacled young lady an authority on all things Russian in the eyes of her immediate set.

'Talk is helpful, talk is needful,' the young man was saying, 'but what we have got to do is to lift the subject out of the furrow of indisciplined talk and place it on the threshing-floor of practical discussion.'

The young woman took advantage of the rhetorical full-stop to dash in with the remark which was already marshalled on the tip of her tongue.

'In emancipating the serfs of poverty we must be careful to avoid the mistakes which Russian bureaucracy stumbled into when liberating the serfs of the soil.'

She paused in her turn for the sake of declamatory effect, but recovered her breath quickly enough to start afresh on level terms with the young man, who had jumped into the stride of his next sentence.

'They got off to a good start that time,' said Francesca to herself; 'I suppose it's the Prevention of Destitution they're hammering at. What on earth would become of these dear good people if anyone started a crusade for the prevention of mediocrity?'

Midway through one of the smaller rooms, still questing for an elusive presence, she caught sight of someone that she knew, and the shadow of a frown passed across her face. The object of her faintly signalled displeasure was Courtenay Youghal, a political spur-winner who seemed absurdly youthful to a generation that had never heard of Pitt. It was Youghal's ambition—or perhaps his hobby—to infuse into the greyness of modern political life some of the colour of Disraelian dandyism, tempered with the correctness of Anglo-Saxon taste, and supplemented by the flashes of wit that were inherent from the Celtic strain in him. His success was only a half-measure. The public missed in him that touch of blatancy which it looks for in its rising public men; the decorative smoothness of his chestnut-golden hair, and the lively sparkle of his epigrams were counted to him for good, but the restrained sumptuousness of his waistcoats and cravats was wasted effort. If he had habitually smoked cigarettes in a pink coral mouthpiece, or worn spats of Mackenzie tartan, the great heart of the voting-man, and the gush of the paragraph-makers might have been unreservedly his. The art of public life consists to a great extent of knowing exactly where to stop and going a bit farther.

It was not Youghal's lack of political sagacity that had brought the momentary look of disapproval into Francesca's face. The fact was that Comus, who had left off being a schoolboy and was now a social problem, had lately enrolled himself among the young politician's associates and admirers, and as the boy knew and cared nothing about politics, and merely copied Youghal's waistcoats, and, less successfully, his conversation, Francesca felt herself justified in deploring the intimacy. To a woman who dressed well on comparatively nothing a year it was an anxious experience to have a son who dressed sumptuously on absolutely nothing.

The cloud that had passed over her face when she caught sight of the offending Youghal was presently succeeded by a smile of gratified achievement as she encountered a bow of recognition and welcome from a portly middle-aged gentleman, who seemed genuinely anxious to include her in the rather meagre group that he had gathered about him.

'We were just talking about my new charge,' he observed genially, including in the 'we' his somewhat depressed-looking listeners, who in all human probability had done none of the talking. 'I was just telling them, and you may be interested to hear this——'

Francesca, with Spartan stoicism, continued to wear an ingratiating smile, though the character of the deaf adder that stoppeth her ear and will not hearken, seemed to her at that moment a beautiful one.

Sir Julian Jull had been a member of a House of Commons

distinguished for its high standard of well-informed mediocrity, and had harmonized so thoroughly with his surroundings that the most attentive observer of Parliamentary proceedings could scarcely have told even on which side of the House he sat. A baronetcy bestowed on him by the Party in power had at least removed that doubt; some weeks later he had been made Governor of some West Indian dependency, whether as a reward for having accepted the baronetcy, or as an application of a theory that West Indian islands get the Governors they deserve, it would have been hard to say. To Sir Julian the appointment was, doubtless, one of some importance; during the span of his Governorship the island might possibly be visited by a member of the Royal Family, or at the least by an earthquake, and in either case his name would get into the papers. To the public the matter was one of absolute indifference; 'who is he and where is it?' would have correctly epitomized the sum total of general information on the personal and geographical aspects of the case.

Francesca, however, from the moment she had heard of the likelihood of the appointment, had taken a deep and lively interest in Sir Julian. As a Member of Parliament he had not filled any very pressing social want in her life, and on the rare occasions when she took tea on the Terrace of the House she was wont to lapse into rapt contemplation of St Thomas's Hospital whenever she saw him within bowing distance. But as Governor of an island he would, of course, want a private secretary, and as a friend and colleague of Henry Greech, to whom he was indebted for many little acts of political support (they had once jointly drafted an amendment which had been ruled out of order), what was more natural and proper than that he should let his choice fall on Henry's nephew Comus? While privately doubting whether the boy would make the sort of secretary that any public man would esteem as a treasure, Henry was thoroughly in agreement with Francesca as to the excellence and desirability of an arrangement which would transplant that troublesome young animal from the too restricted and conspicuous area that centres in the parish of St James's to some misty corner of the British dominion overseas. Brother and sister had conspired to give an elaborate and at the same time cosy little luncheon to Sir Julian on the very day that his appointment was officially announced, and the question of the secretaryship had been mooted and sedulously fostered as occasion permitted, until all that was now needed to clinch the matter was a formal interview between His Excellency and Comus. The boy had from the first shown very little gratification at the prospect of his deportation. To live on a remote shark-girt island, as he expressed it, with the Jull family as his chief social mainstay, and Sir Julian's conversation as a daily item of his existence, did not inspire him with the same degree of enthusiasm as was displayed by his mother and uncle, who, after all, were not making the experiment. Even the necessity for an entirely new outfit did not appeal to his imagination with the force that might have been expected. But, however lukewarm his adhesion to the project might be, Francesca and her brother were clearly determined that no lack of deft persistence on their part should endanger its success. It was for the purpose of reminding Sir Julian of his promise to meet Comus at lunch on the following day, and definitely settle the matter of the secretaryship, that Francesca was now enduring the ordeal of a long harangue on the value of the West Indian group as an Imperial asset. Other listeners dexterously detached themselves one by one, but Francesca's patience outlasted even Sir Julian's flow of commonplaces, and her devotion was duly rewarded by a renewed acknowledgment of the lunch engagement and its purpose. She pushed her way back through the throng of starling-voiced chatterers fortified by a sense of well-earned victory. Dear Serena's absurd *salons* served some good purpose after all.

Francesca was not an early riser, and her breakfast was only just beginning to mobilize on the breakfast-table next morning when a copy of *The Times*, sent by special messenger from her brother's house, was brought up to her room. A heavy margin of blue pencilling drew her attention to a prominently-printed letter which bore the ironical heading: 'Julian Jull, Proconsul.' The matter of the letter was a cruel disinterment of some fatuous and forgotten speeches made by Sir Julian to his constituents not many years ago, in which the value of some of our Colonial possessions, particularly certain West Indian islands, was decried in a medley of pomposity, ignorance and amazingly cheap humour. The extracts given sounded weak and foolish enough, taken by themselves, but the writer of the letter had interlarded them with comments of his own, which sparkled with an ironical brilliance that was Cervantes-like in its polished cruelty. Remembering her ordeal of the previous evening Francesca permitted herself a certain feeling of amusement as she read the merciless stabs inflicted on the newly-appointed Governor; then she came to the signature at the foot of the letter and the laughter died out of her eyes. 'Comus Bassington' stared at her from above a thick layer of blue pencil lines marked by Henry Greech's shaking hand.

Comus could no more have devised such a letter than he could have written an Episcopal charge to the clergy of any given diocese. It was obviously the work of Courtenay Youghal, and Comus, for a palpable purpose of his own, had wheedled him into forgoing for once the pride of authorship in a clever piece of political raillery, and letting his young friend stand sponsor instead. It was a daring stroke, and there could be no question as to its success; the secretaryship and the distant shark-girt island faded away into the horizon of impossible things. Francesca, forgetting the golden rule of strategy which enjoins a careful choosing of ground and opportunity before entering on hostilities, made straight for the bathroom door, behind which a lively din of splashing betokened that Comus had at least begun his toilet.

'You wicked boy, what have you done?' she cried reproachfully.

'Me washee,' came a cheerful shout; 'me washee from the neck all the way down to the merrythought, and now washee down from the merrythought to——'

'You have ruined your future. *The Times* has printed that miserable letter with your signature.'

A loud squeal of joy came from the bath. 'Oh, Mummy! Let me see!'

There were sounds as of a sprawling dripping body clambering hastily out of the bath. Francesca fled. One cannot effectively scold a moist nineteen-year-old boy clad only in a bath-towel and a cloud of steam.

Another messenger arrived before Francesca's breakfast was over. This one brought a letter from Sir Julian Jull, excusing himself from fulfilment of the luncheon engagement.

CHAPTER IV

FRANCESCA prided herself on being able to see things from other people's points of view, which meant, as it usually does, that she could see her own point of view from various aspects. As regards Comus, whose doings and non-doings bulked largely in her thoughts at the present moment, she had mapped out in her mind so clearly what his outlook in life ought to be, that she was peculiarly unfitted to understand the drift of his feelings or the impulses that governed them. Fate had endowed her with a son; in limiting the endowment to a solitary offspring Fate had certainly shown a moderation which Francesca was perfectly willing to acknowledge and be thankful for; but then, as she pointed out to a certain complacent friend of hers who cheerfully sustained an endowment of half a dozen male offsprings and a girl or two, her one child was Comus. Moderation in numbers was more than counterbalanced in his case by extravagance in characteristics.

Francesca mentally compared her son with hundreds of other young men whom she saw around her, steadily, and no doubt happily, engaged in the process of transforming themselves from nice boys into useful citizens. Most of them had occupations, or were industriously engaged in qualifying for such; in their leisure moments they smoked reasonably-priced cigarettes, went to the cheaper seats at music-halls, watched an occasional cricket match at Lord's with apparent interest, saw most of the world's spectacular events through the medium of the cinematograph, and were wont to exchange at parting seemingly superfluous injunctions to 'be good'. The whole of Bond Street and many of the tributary thoroughfares of Piccadilly might have been swept off the face of modern London without in any way interfering with the supply of their daily wants. They were doubtless dull as acquaintances, but as sons they would have been eminently restful. With a growing sense of irritation Francesca compared these deserving young men with her own intractable offspring, and wondered why Fate should have singled her out to be the parent of such a vexatious variant from a comfortable and desirable type. As far as remunerative achievement was concerned, Comus copied the insouciance of the field lily with a dangeous fidelity. Like his mother he looked round with wistful irritation at the example afforded by contemporary youth, but he concentrated his attention exclusively on the richer circles of his acquaintance, young men who bought cars and polo ponies as unconcernedly as he might purchase a carnation for his buttonhole, and went for trips to Cairo or the Tigris valley with less difficulty and finance-stretching than he encountered in contriving a week-end at Brighton.

Gaiety and good looks had carried Comus successfully and, on the whole, pleasantly, through schooldays and a recurring succession of holidays; the same desirable assets were still at his service to advance him along his road, but it was a disconcerting experience to find that they could not be relied on to go all distances at all times. In an animal world, and a fiercely competitive animal world at that, something more was needed than the decorative *abandon* of the field lily, and it was just that something more which Comus seemed unable or unwilling to provide on his own account; it was just the lack of that something more which left him sulking with Fate over the numerous breakdowns and stumbling-blocks that held him up on what he expected to be a triumphal or, at any rate, unimpeded progress.

Francesca was, in her own way, fonder of Comus than of anyone else in the world, and if he had been browning his skin somewhere east of Suez she would probably have kissed his photograph with genuine fervour every night before going to bed; the appearance of a cholera scare or rumour of native rising in the columns of her daily news-sheet would have caused her a flutter of anxiety, and she would have mentally likened herself to a Spartan mother sacrificing her best-beloved on the altar of State necessities. But with the best-loved installed under her roof, occupying an unreasonable amount of cubic space, and demanding daily sacrifices instead of providing the raw material for one, her feelings were tinged with irritation rather than affection. She might have forgiven Comus generously for misdeeds of some gravity committed in another continent, but she could never overlook the fact that out of a dish of five plovers' eggs he was certain to take three. The absent

36

may be always wrong, but they are seldom in a position to be inconsiderate.

Thus a wall of ice had grown up gradually between mother and son, a barrier across which they could hold converse, but which gave a wintry chill even to the sparkle of their lightest words. The boy had the gift of being irresistibly amusing when he chose to exert himself in that direction, and after a long series of moody or jangling meal-sittings he would break forth into a torrential flow of small talk, scandal and malicious anecdote, true or more generally invented, to which Francesca listened with a relish and appreciation that was all the more flattering from being so unwillingly bestowed.

'If you chose your friends from a rather more reputable set you would be doubtless less amusing, but there would be compensating advantages.'

Francesca snapped the remark out at lunch one day when she had been betrayed into a broader smile than she considered the circumstances of her attitude towards Comus warranted.

'I'm going to move in quite decent society tonight,' replied Comus with a pleased chuckle; 'I'm going to meet you and Uncle Henry and heaps of nice dull God-fearing people at dinner.'

Francesca gave a little gasp of surprise and annoyance.

'You don't mean to say Caroline has asked you to dinner tonight?' she said; 'and of course without telling me. How exceedingly like her!'

Lady Caroline Benaresq had reached that age when you can say and do what you like in defiance of people's most sensitive feelings and most cherished antipathies. Not that she had waited to attain her present age before pursuing that line of conduct; she came of a family whose individual members went through life, from the nursery to the grave, with as much tact and consideration as a cactus-hedge might show in going through a crowded bathing tent. It was a compensating mercy that they disagreed rather more among themselves than they did with the outside world; every known variety and shade of religion and politics had been pressed into the family service to avoid the possibility of any agreement on the larger essentials of life, and such unlooked-for happenings as the Home Rule schism, the Tariff-Reform upheaval and the

Suffragette crusade were thankfully seized on as furnishing occasion for further differences and subdivisions. Lady Caroline's favourite scheme of entertaining was to bring jarring and antagonistic elements into close contact and play them remorselessly one against the other. 'One gets much better results under those circumstances,' she used to observe, 'than by asking people who wish to meet each other. Few people talk as brilliantly to impress a friend as they do to depress an enemy.'

She admitted that her theory broke down rather badly if you applied it to Parliamentary debates. At her own dinner table its success was usually triumphantly vindicated.

'Who else is to be there?' Francesca asked, with some pardonable misgiving.

'Courtenay Youghal. He'll probably sit next to you, so you'd better think out a lot of annihilating remarks in readiness. And Elaine de Frey.'

'I don't think I've heard of her. Who is she?'

'Nobody in particular, but rather nice looking in a solemn sort of way, and almost indecently rich.'

'Marry her' was the advice which sprang to Francesca's lips, but she choked it back with a salted almond, having a rare perception of the fact that words are sometimes given to us to defeat our purposes.

'Caroline has probably marked her down for Toby or one of the grand-nephews,' she said carelessly; 'a little money would be rather useful in that quarter, I imagine.'

Comus tucked in his underlip with just the shade of pugnacity that she wanted to see.

An advantageous marriage was so obviously the most sensible course for him to embark on that she scarcely dared to hope that he would seriously entertain it; yet there was just a chance that if he got as far as the flirtation stage with an attractive (and attracted) girl who was also an heiress, the sheer perversity of his nature might carry him on to more definite courtship, if only from the desire to thrust other more genuinely enamoured suitors into the background. It was a forlorn hope; so forlorn that the idea even crossed her mind of throwing herself on the mercy of her *bête noire*, Courtenay Youghal, and trying to enlist the influence which he seemed to possess over Comus for the purpose of furthering her hurriedly conceived project. Anyhow, the dinner promised to be more interesting than she had originally anticipated.

Lady Caroline was a professed Socialist in politics, chiefly, it was believed, because she was thus enabled to disagree with most of the Liberals and Conservatives, and all the Socialists of the day. She did not permit her Socialism, however, to penetrate below stairs; her cook and butler had every encouragement to be Individualists. Francesca, who was a keen and intelligent food critic, harboured no misgivings as to her hostess's kitchen and cellar departments; some of the human side-dishes at the feast gave her more ground for uneasiness. Courtenay Youghal, for instance, would probably be brilliantly silent; her brother Henry would almost certainly be the reverse.

The dinner party was a large one, and Francesca arrived late with little time to take preliminary stock of the guests; a card with the name 'Miss de Frey,' immediately opposite her own place at the other side of the table, indicated, however, the whereabouts of the heiress. It was characteristic of Francesca that she first carefully read the menu from end to end, and then indulged in an equally careful, though less open, scrutiny of the girl who sat opposite her, the girl who was nobody in particular, but whose income was everything that could be desired. She was pretty in a restrained nut-brown fashion, and had a look of grave reflective calm that probably masked a speculative unsettled temperament. Her pose, if one wished to be critical, was just a little too elaborately careless. She wore some excellently set rubies with that indefinable air of having more at home that is so difficult to improvise. Francesca was distinctly pleased with her survey.

'You seem interested in your *vis-à-vis*,' said Courtenay Youghal.

'I almost think I've seen her before,' said Francesca; 'her face seems familiar to me.'

'The narrow gallery at the Louvre: attributed to Leonardo da Vinci,' said Youghal.

'Of course,' said Francesca, her feelings divided between satisfaction at capturing an elusive impression and annoyance that Youghal should have been her helper. A stronger tinge of annoyance possessed her when she heard the voice of Henry Greech raised in painful prominence at Lady Caroline's end of the table.

'I called on the Trudhams yesterday,' he announced; 'it was their Silver Wedding, you know, at least the day before was. Such lots of silver presents, quite a show. Of course there were a great many duplicates, but still, very nice to have. I think they were very pleased to get so many.'

'We must not grudge them their show of presents after their twenty-five years of married life,' said Lady Caroline gently; 'it is the silver lining to their cloud.'

A third of the guests present were related to the Trudhams.

'Lady Caroline is beginning well,' murmured Courtenay Youghal.

'I should hardly call twenty-five years of married life a cloud,' said Henry Greech lamely.

'Don't let's talk about married life,' said a tall handsome woman, who looked like some modern painter's conception of the goddess Bellona; 'it's my misfortune to write eternally about husbands and wives and their variants. My public expects it of me. I do so envy journalists who can write about plagues and strikes and Anarchist plots, and other pleasing things, instead of being tied down to one stale old topic.'

'Who is that woman and what has she written?' Francesca asked Youghal; she dimly remembered having seen her at one of Serena Golackly's gatherings, surrounded by a little court of admirers.

'I forget her name; she has a villa at San Remo or Mentone, or somewhere where one does have villas, and plays an extraordinary good game of bridge. Also she has the reputation, rather rare in your sex, of being a wonderfully sound judge of wine.'

'But what has she written?'

'Oh, several novels of the thinnish ice order. Her last one, *The Woman Who Wished it was Wednesday*, has been banned at all the libraries. I expect you've read it.'

'I don't see why you should think so,' said Francesca coldly.

'Only because Comus lent me your copy yesterday,' said Youghal. He threw back his handsome head and gave her a sidelong glance of quizzical amusement. He knew that she hated his intimacy with Comus, and he was secretly rather proud of his influence over the boy, shallow and negative though he knew it to be. It had been, on his part, an unsought intimacy, and it would probably fall to pieces the moment he tried seriously to take up the *rôle* of mentor. The fact that Comus's mother openly disapproved of the friendship gave it perhaps its chief interest in the young politician's eyes.

Francesca turned her attention to her brother's end of the table. Henry Greech had willingly availed himself of the invitation to leave the subject of married life, and had launched forthwith into the equally well-worn theme of current politics. He was not a person who was in much demand for public meetings, and the House showed no great impatience to hear his views on the topics of the moment; its impatience, indeed, was manifested rather in the opposite direction. Hence he was prone to unburden himself of accumulated political wisdom as occasion presented itself— sometimes, indeed, to assume an occasion that was hardly visible to the naked intelligence.

'Our opponents are engaged in a hopelessly uphill struggle, and they know it,' he chirruped defiantly; 'they've become possessed, like the Gadarene swine, with a whole legion of——'

'Surely the Gadarene swine went down-hill?' put in Lady Caroline in a gently inquiring voice.

Henry Greech hastily abandoned simile and fell back on platitude and the safer kinds of fact.

Francesca did not regard her brother's views on statecraft either in the light of gospel or revelation; as Comus once remarked, they more usually suggested exodus. In the present instance she found distraction in a renewed scrutiny of the girl opposite her, who seemed to be only moderately interested in the conversational efforts of the diners on either side of her. Comus, who was looking and talking his best, was sitting at the farther end of the table, and Francesca was quick to notice in which direction the girl's glances were continually straying. Once or twice the eyes of the young people met and a swift flush of pleasure and a half-smile that spoke of good understanding came to the heiress's face. It did not need the gift of the traditional intuition of her sex to enable Francesca to guess that the girl with the desirable banking account was already considerably attracted by the lively young Pagan who had, when he cared to practise it, such an art of winning admiration. For the first time for many, many months Francesca saw her son's prospects in a rose-coloured setting, and she began, unconsciously, to wonder exactly how much wealth was summed up in the expressive label 'almost indecently rich'. A wife with a really large fortune and a correspondingly big dower of character and ambition, might, perhaps, succeed in turning Comus's latent energies into a groove which would provide him, if not with a career, at least with an occupation, and the young serious face opposite looked as if its owner lacked neither character nor ambition. Francesca's speculations took a more personal turn. Out of the well-filled coffers with which her imagination was toying, an inconsiderable sum might eventually be devoted to the leasing, or even perhaps the purchase of, the house in Blue Street when the present convenient arrangement should have come to an end, and Francesca and the Van der Meulen would not be obliged to seek fresh quarters.

A woman's voice, talking in a discreet undertone on the other side of Courtenay Youghal, broke in on her bridge-building.

'Tons of money and really very presentable. Just the wife for a rising young politician. Go in and win her before she's snapped up by some fortune hunter.'

Youghal and his instructress in worldly wisdom were looking straight across the table at the Leonardo da Vinci girl with the grave reflective eyes and the over-emphasized air of repose. Francesca felt a quick throb of anger against her matchmaking neighbour; why, she asked herself, must some women, with no end or purpose of their own to serve, except the sheer love of meddling in the affairs of others, plunge their hands into plots and schemings of this sort, in which the happiness of more than one person was concerned? And more clearly than ever she realized how thoroughly she detested Courtenay Youghal. She had disliked him as an evil influence, setting before her son an example of showy ambition that he was not in the least likely to follow, and providing him with a model of extravagant dandyism that he was only too certain to copy. In her heart she knew that Comus would have embarked just as surely on his present course of idle self-indulgence if he had never known of the existence of Youghal, but she chose to regard that young man as her son's evil genius, and now he seemed likely to justify more than ever the character she had fastened on to him. For once in his life Comus appeared to

42

have an idea of behaving sensibly and making some use of his opportunities, and almost at the same moment Courtenay Youghal arrived on the scene as a possible and very dangerous rival. Against the good looks and fitful powers of fascination that Comus could bring into the field, the young politician could match half a dozen dazzling qualities which would go far to recommend him in the eyes of a woman of the world, still more in those of a young girl in search of an ideal. Good-looking in his own way, if not on such showy lines as Comus, always well turned-out, witty, self-confident without being bumptious, with a conspicuous Parliamentary career alongside him, and Heaven knew what else in front of him, Courtenay Youghal certainly was not a rival whose chances could be held very lightly. Francesca laughed bitterly to herself as she remembered that a few hours ago she had entertained the idea of begging for his good offices in helping on Comus's wooing. One consolation, at least, she found for herself: if Youghal really meant to step in and try and cut out his young friend, the latter at any rate had snatched a useful start. Comus had mentioned Miss de Frey at luncheon that day, casually and dispassionately; if the subject of the dinner guests had not come up he would probably not have mentioned her at all. But they were obviously already very good friends. It was part and parcel of the state of domestic tension at Blue Street that Francesca should only have come to know of this highly interesting heiress by an accidental sorting of guests at a dinner party.

Lady Caroline's voice broke in on her reflections; it was a gentle purring voice, that possessed an uncanny quality of being able to make itself heard down the longest dinner table.

'The dear Archdeacon is getting *so* absent-minded. He read a list of box-holders for the opera as the First Lesson the other Sunday, instead of the families and lots of the tribes of Israel that entered Canaan. Fortunately no one noticed the mistake.'

CHAPTER V

ON a conveniently secluded bench facing the Northern Pheasantry in the Zoological Society's Gardens, Regent's Park,
Courtenay Youghal sat immersed in mature flirtation with a lady,
who, though certainly young in fact and appearance, was some four
or five years his senior. When he was a schoolboy of sixteen, Molly
McQuade had personally conducted him to the Zoo and stood
him dinner afterwards at Kettner's, and whenever the two of them
happened to be in town on the anniversary of that bygone festivity
they religiously repeated the programme in its entirety. Even the
menu of the dinner was adhered to as nearly as possible; the original
selection of food and wine that schoolboy exuberance, tempered
by schoolboy shyness, had pitched on those many years ago, confronted Youghal on those occasions, as a drowning man's past life
is said to rise up and parade itself in his last moments of consciousness.

The flirtation which was thus perennially restored to its old-
time footing owed its longevity more to the enterprising solicitude
of Miss McQuade than to any conscious sentimental effort on the
part of Youghal himself. Molly McQuade was known to her
neighbours in a minor hunting shire as a hard-riding conventionally
unconventional type of young woman, who came naturally into
the classification, 'a good sort'. She was just sufficiently good-
looking, sufficiently reticent about her own illnesses, when she had
any, and sufficiently appreciative of her neighbours' gardens,
children and hunters to be generally popular. Most men liked her,
and the percentage of women who disliked her was not incon-
veniently high. One of these days, it was assumed, she would
marry a brewer or a Master of Otter Hounds, and, after a brief
interval, be known to the world as the mother of a boy or
two at Malvern or some similar seat of learning. The romantic
side of her nature was altogether unguessed by the countryside.

Her romances were mostly in serial form, and suffered perhaps

44

in fervour from their disconnected course what they gained in length of days. Her affectionate interest in the several young men who figured in her affairs of the heart was perfectly honest, and she certainly made no attempt either to conceal their separate existences, or to play them off one against the other. Neither could it be said that she was a husband hunter; she had made up her mind what sort of man she was likely to marry, and her forecast did not differ very widely from that formed by her local acquaintances. If her married life were eventually to turn out a failure, at least she looked forward to it with very moderate expectations. Her love affairs she put on a very different footing, and apparently they were the all-absorbing element in her life. She possessed the happily constituted temperament which enables a man or woman to be a 'pluralist', and to observe the sage precaution of not putting all one's eggs into one basket. Her demands were not exacting; she required of her affinity that he should be young, good-looking, and at least moderately amusing; she would have preferred him to be invariably faithful, but, with her own example before her, she was prepared for the probability, bordering on certainty, that he would be nothing of the sort. The philosophy of the 'Garden of Kama' was the compass by which she steered her barque, and thus far, if she had encountered some storms and buffeting, she had at least escaped being either shipwrecked or becalmed.

Courtenay Youghal had not been designed by Nature to fulfil the *rôle* of an ardent or devoted lover, and he scrupulously respected the limits which Nature had laid down. For Molly, however, he had a certain responsive affection. She had always obviously admired him, and at the same time she never beset him with crude flattery; the principal reason why the flirtation had stood the test of so many years was the fact that it only flared into active existence at convenient intervals. In an age when the telephone has undermined almost every fastness of human privacy, and the sanctity of one's seclusion depends often on the ability for tactful falsehood shown by a club pageboy, Youghal was duly appreciative of the circumstance that his lady fair spent a large part of the year pursuing foxes, in lieu of pursuing him. Also the honestly admitted fact that, in her human hunting, she rode after more than one quarry, made the inevitable break-up of the affair a matter to which both could look forward without a sense of coming embarrassment and recrimination. When the time for gathering ye rosebuds should be over, neither of them could accuse the other of having wrecked his or her entire life. At the most they would only have disorganized a week-end.

On this particular afternoon, when old reminiscences had been gone through, and the intervening gossip of past months duly recounted, a lull in the conversation made itself rather obstinately felt. Molly had already guessed that matters were about to slip into a new phase; the affair had reached maturity along ago, and a new phase must be in the nature of a wane.

'You're a clever brute,' she said suddenly, with an air of affectionate regret; 'I always knew you'd get on in the House, but I hardly expected you to come to the front so soon.'

'I'm coming to the front,' admitted Youghal judicially; 'the problem is, shall I be able to stay there? Unless something happens in the financial line before long, I don't see how I'm to stay in Parliament at all. Economy is out of the question. It would open people's eyes, I fancy, if they knew how little I exist on as it is. And I'm living so far beyond my income that we may almost be said to be living apart.'

'It will have to be a rich wife, I suppose,' said Molly slowly; 'that's the worst of success, it imposes so many conditions. I rather knew, from something in your manner, that you were drifting that way.'

Youghal said nothing in the way of contradiction; he gazed steadfastly at the aviary in front of him as though exotic pheasants were for the moment the most absorbing study in the world. As a matter of fact, his mind was centred on the image of Elaine de Frey, with her clear untroubled eyes and her Leonardo da Vinci air. He was wondering whether he was likely to fall into a frame of mind concerning her which would be in the least like falling in love.

'I shall mind horribly,' continued Molly, after a pause, 'but, of course, I have always known that something of the sort would have to happen one of these days. When a man goes into politics he can't call his soul his own, and I suppose his heart becomes an impersonal possession in the same way.'

46

'Most people who know me would tell you that I haven't got a heart,' said Youghal.

'I've often felt inclined to agree with them,' said Molly; 'and then, now and again, I think you have a heart tucked away somewhere.'

'I hope I have,' said Youghal, 'because I'm trying to break to you the fact that I think I'm falling in love with somebody.'

Molly McQuade turned sharply to look at her companion, who still fixed his gaze on the pheasant run in front of him.

'Don't tell me you're losing your head over somebody useless, someone without money,' she said; 'I don't think I could stand that.'

For the moment she feared that Courtenay's selfishness might have taken an unexpected turn, in which ambition had given way to the fancy of the hour; he might be going to sacrifice his Parliamentary career for a life of stupid lounging in momentarily attractive company. He quickly undeceived her.

'She's got heaps of money.'

Molly gave a grunt of relief. Her affection for Courtenay had produced the anxiety which underlay her first question; a natural jealousy prompted the next one.

'Is she young and pretty and all that sort of thing, or is she just a good sort with a sympathetic manner and nice eyes? As a rule that's the kind that goes with a lot of money.'

'Young and quite good-looking in her way, and a distinct style of her own. Some people would call her beautiful. As a political hostess I should think she'd be splendid. I imagine I'm rather in love with her.'

'And is she in love with you?'

Youghal threw back his head with the slight assertive movement that Molly knew and liked.

'She's a girl who I fancy would let judgment influence her a lot. And without being stupidly conceited I think I may say she might do worse than throw herself away on me. I'm young and quite good-looking, and I'm making a name for myself in the House; she'll be able to read all sorts of nice and horrid things about me in the papers at breakfast-time. I can be brilliantly amusing at times, and I understand the value of silence; there is no fear that

I shall ever degenerate into that fearsome thing—a cheerful talkative husband. For a girl with money and social ambitions I should think I was rather a good thing.'

'You are certainly in love, Courtenay,' said Molly, 'but it's the old love and not a new one. I'm rather glad. I should have hated to have you head-over-heels in love with a pretty woman, even for a short time. You'll be much happier as it is. And I'm going to put all my feelings in the background, and tell you to go in and win. You've got to marry a rich woman, and if she's nice and will make a good hostess, so much the better for everybody. You'll be happier in your married life than I shall be in mine, when it comes; you'll have other interests to absorb you. I shall just have the garden and dairy and nursery and lending library, as like as two peas to all the gardens and dairies and nurseries for hundreds of miles round. You won't care for your wife enough to be worried every time she has a finger-ache, and you'll like her well enough to be pleased to meet her sometimes at your own house. I shouldn't wonder if you were quite happy. She will probably be miserable, but any woman who married you would be.'

There was a short pause; they were both staring at the pheasant cages. Then Molly spoke again, with the swift nervous tone of a general who is hurriedly altering the disposition of his forces for a strategic retreat.

'When you are safely married and honeymooned and all that sort of thing, and have put your wife through her paces as a political hostess, some time, when the House isn't sitting, you must come down by yourself, and do a little hunting with us. Will you? It won't be quite the same as old times, but it will be something to look forward to when I'm reading the endless paragraphs about your fashionable political wedding.'

'You're looking forward pretty far,' laughed Youghal; 'the lady may take your view as to the probable unhappiness of a future shared with me, and I may have to content myself with penurious political bachelorhood. Anyhow, the present is still with us. We dine at Kettner's to-night, don't we?'

'Rather,' said Molly, 'though it will be more or less a throat-lumpy feast as far as I am concerned. We shall have to drink to the health of the future Mrs Youghal. By the way, it's rather characteristic of you that you haven't told me who she is, and of me that I haven't asked. And now, like a dear boy, trot away and leave me. I haven't got to say good-bye to you yet, but I'm going to take a quiet farewell of the Pheasantry. We've had some jolly good talks, you and I, sitting on this seat, haven't we? And I know, as well as I know anything, that this is the last of them. Eight o'clock to-night, as punctually as possible.'

She watched his retreating figure with eyes that grew slowly misty; he had been such a jolly comely boy-friend, and they had had such good times together. The mist deepened on her lashes as she looked round at the familiar rendezvous where they had so often kept tryst since the day when they had first come there together, he a schoolboy and she but lately out of her teens. For the moment she felt herself in the thrall of a very real sorrow.

Then, with the admirable energy of one who is only in town for a fleeting fortnight, she raced away to have tea with a world-faring naval admirer at his club. Pluralism is a merciful narcotic.

CHAPTER VI

ELAINE DE FREY sat at ease—at bodily ease, at any rate—in a low wicker chair placed under the shade of a group of cedars in the heart of a stately spacious garden that had almost made up its mind to be a park. The shallow stone basin of an old fountain, on whose wide ledge a leaden-moulded otter for ever preyed on a leaden salmon, filled a conspicuous place in the immediate foreground. Around its rim ran an inscription in Latin, warning mortal man that time flows as swiftly as water and exhorting him to make the most of his hours; after which piece of Jacobean moralizing it set itself shamelessly to beguile all who might pass that way into an abandonment of contemplative repose. On all sides of it a stretch of smooth turf spread away, broken up here and there by groups of dwarfish chestnut and mulberry trees, whose leaves and branches cast a laced pattern of shade beneath them. On one side the lawn sloped gently down to a small lake, whereon floated a quartette of swans, their movements suggestive of a certain mournful listlessness, as though a weary dignity of caste held them back from the joyous bustling life of the lesser waterfowl. Elaine liked to imagine that they re-embodied the souls of unhappy boys who had been forced by family interests to become high ecclesiastical dignitaries and had grown prematurely Right Reverend. A low stone balustrade fenced part of the shore of the lake, making a miniature terrace above its level, and here roses grew in a rich multitude. Other rose bushes, carefully pruned and tended, formed little oases of colour and perfume amid the restful green of the sward, and in the distance the eye caught the variegated blaze of a many-hued hedge of rhododendron. With these favoured exceptions flowers were hard to find in this well-ordered garden; the misguided tyranny of staring geranium beds and beflowered archways leading to nowhere, so dear to the suburban gardener, found no expression here. Magnificent Amherst pheasants, whose plumage challenged and almost shamed the peacock on his own ground, stepped to and fro over the emerald turf with the assured self-conscious pride of reigning sultans. It was a garden where summer seemed a part-proprietor rather than a hurried visitor.

By the side of Elaine's chair under the shadow of the cedars a wicker table was set out with the paraphernalia of afternoon tea. On some cushions at her feet reclined Courtenay Youghal, smoothly preened and youthfully elegant, the personification of decorative repose. Equally decorative, but with the showy restlessness of a dragonfly. Comus disported his flannelled person over a considerable span of the available foreground.

The intimacy existing between the two young men had suffered no immediate dislocation from the circumstance that they were tacitly paying court to the same lady. It was an intimacy founded not in the least on friendship or community of tastes and ideas, but owed its existence to the fact that each was amused and interested by the other. Youghal found Comus, for the time being at any rate, just as amusing and interesting as a rival for Elaine's favour as he had been in the *rôle* of scapegrace boy-about-town; Comus for his part did not wish to lose touch with Youghal, who among other attractions possessed the recommendation of being under the ban of Comus's mother. She disapproved, it is true, of a great many of her son's friends and associates, but this particular one was a special and persistent source of irritation to her from the fact that he figured prominently and more or less successfully in the public life of the day. There was something peculiarly exasperating in reading a brilliant and incisive attack on the Government's rash handling of public expenditure delivered by a young man who encouraged her son in every imaginable extravagance. The actual extent of Youghal's influence over the boy was of the slightest; Comus was quite capable of deriving encouragement to rash outlay and frivolous conversation from an anchorite or an East End parson if he had been thrown into close companionship with such an individual. Francesca, however, exercised a mother's privilege in assuming her son's bachelor associates to be industrious in labouring to achieve his undoing. Therefore the young politician was a source of unconcealed annoyance to her, and in the same degree as she expressed her disapproval of him Comus was careful to maintain and parade the intimacy. Its existence, or rather its continued existence, was one of the things that faintly puzzled the young lady whose sought-for favour might have been expected to furnish an occasion for its rapid dissolution.

With two suitors, one of whom at least she found markedly attractive, courting her at the same moment, Elaine should have had reasonable cause for being on good terms with the world, and with herself in particular. Happiness was not, however, at this auspicious moment, her dominant mood. The grave calm of her face masked as usual a certain degree of grave perturbation. A succession of well-meaning governesses and a plentiful supply of moralizing aunts on both sides of her family, had impressed on her young mind the theoretical fact that wealth is a great responsibility. The consciousness of her responsibility set her continually wondering, not as to her own fitness to discharge her 'stewardship', but as to the motives and merits of people with whom she came in contact. The knowledge that there was so much in the world that she could buy, invited speculation as to how much there was that was worth buying. Gradually she had come to regard her mind as a sort of appeal court before whose secret sittings were examined and judged the motives and actions, the motives especially, of the world in general. In her schoolroom days she had sat in conscientious judgment on the motives that guided or misguided Charles and Cromwell and Monck, Wallenstein and Savonarola. In her present stage she was equally occupied in examining the political sincerity of the Secretary for Foreign Affairs, the good-faith of a honey-tongued but possibly loyal-hearted waiting-maid, and the disinterestedness of a whole circle of indulgent and flattering acquaintances. Even more absorbing, and, in her eyes, more urgently necessary, was the task of dissecting and appraising the characters of the two young men who were favouring her with their attentions. And herein lay cause for much thinking and some perturbation. Youghal, for example, might have baffled a more experienced observer of human nature. Elaine was too clever to confound his dandyism with foppishness or self-advertisement. He admired his own toilet effect in a mirror from a genuine sense of pleasure in a thing good to look upon, just as he would feel a sensuous appreciation of the sight of a well-bred, well-matched, well-turned-out pair of horses. Behind his careful political flippancy and cynicism one might also detect a certain careless sincerity, which would probably in the long run save him from moderate success, and turn him into one of the brilliant failures of his day. Beyond this it was difficult to form an exact appreciation of Courtenay Youghal, and Elaine, who liked to have her impressions distinctly labelled and pigeon-holed, was perpetually scrutinizing the outer surface of his characteristics and utterances, like a baffled art critic vainly searching beneath the varnish and scratches of a doubtfully assigned picture for an enlightening signature. The young man added to her perplexities by his deliberate policy of never trying to show himself in a favourable light even when most anxious to impart a favourable impression. He preferred that people should hunt for his good qualities, and merely took very good care that as far as possible they should never draw blank; even in the matter of selfishness, which was the anchor-sheet of his existence, he contrived to be noted, and justly noted, for doing remarkably unselfish things. As a ruler he would have been reasonably popular; as a husband he would probably be unendurable.

Comus was to a certain extent as great a mystification as Youghal, but here Elaine was herself responsible for some of the perplexity which enshrouded his character in her eyes. She had taken more than a passing fancy for the boy—for the boy as he might be, that was to say—and she was desperately unwilling to see him and appraise him as he really was. Thus the mental court of appeal was constantly engaged in examining witnesses as to character, most of whom signally failed to give any testimony which would support the favourable judgment which the tribunal was so anxious to arrive at. A woman with wider experience of the world's ways and shortcomings would probably have contented herself with an endeavour to find out whether her liking for the boy outweighed her dislike of his characteristics; Elaine took her judgments too seriously to approach the matter from such a simple and convenient standpoint. The fact that she was much more than half in love with Comus made it dreadfully important that she should discover him to have a lovable soul, and Comus, it must be confessed, did little to help forward the discovery.

'At any rate he is honest,' she would observe to herself, after

53

some outspoken admission of unprincipled conduct on his part, and then she would ruefully recall certain episodes in which he had figured, from which honesty had been conspicuously absent. What she tried to label honesty in his candour was probably only a cynical defiance of the laws of right and wrong.

'You look more than usually thoughtful this afternoon,' said Comus to her, 'as if you had invented this summer day and were trying to think out improvements.'

'If I had the power to create improvements anywhere I think I should begin with you,' retorted Elaine.

'I'm sure it's much better to leave me as I am,' protested Comus; 'you're like a relative of mine up in Argyllshire, who spends his time producing improved breeds of sheep and pigs and chickens. So patronizing and irritating to the Almighty, I should think, to go about putting superior finishing touches to Creation.'

Elaine frowned, and then laughed, and finally gave a little sigh.

'It's not easy to talk sense to you,' she said.

'Whatever else you take in hand,' said Youghal, 'you must never improve this garden. It's what our idea of heaven might be like if the Jews hadn't invented one for us on totally different lines. It's dreadful that we should accept them as the impresarios of our religious dreamland instead of the Greeks.'

'You are not very fond of the Jews,' said Elaine.

'I've travelled and lived a good deal in Eastern Europe,' said Youghal.

'It seems largely a question of geography,' said Elaine; 'in England no one really is anti-Semitic.'

Youghal shook his head. 'I know a great many Jews who are.'

Servants had quietly, almost reverently, placed tea and its accessories on the wicker table, and quietly receded from the landscape. Elaine sat like a grave young goddess about to dispense some mysterious potion to her devotees. Her mind was still sitting in judgment on the Jewish question.

Comus scrambled to his feet.

'It's too hot for tea,' he said; 'I shall go and feed the swans.'

And he walked off with a little silver basket-dish containing brown bread-and-butter.

Elaine laughed quietly.

'It's so like Comus,' she said, 'to go off with our one dish of bread-and-butter.'

Youghal chuckled responsively. It was an undoubted opportunity for him to put in some disparaging criticism of Comus, and Elaine sat alert in readiness to judge the critic and reserve judgment on the criticized.

'His selfishness is splendid but absolutely futile,' said Youghal; 'now my selfishness is commonplace, but always thoroughly practical and calculated. He will have great difficulty in getting the swans to accept his offering, and he incurs the odium of reducing us to a bread-and-butterless condition. Incidentally, he will get very hot.'

Elaine again had the sense of being thoroughly baffled. If Youghal had said anything unkind it was about himself.

'If my cousin Suzette had been here,' she observed, with the shadow of a malicious smile on her lips, 'I believe she would have gone into a flood of tears at the loss of her bread-and-butter, and Comus would have figured ever after in her mind as something black and destroying and hateful. In fact, I don't really know why we took our loss so unprotestingly.'

'For two reasons,' said Youghal; 'you are rather fond of Comus. And I—am not very fond of bread-and-butter.'

The jesting remark brought a throb of pleasure to Elaine's heart. She had known full well that she cared for Comus, but now that Courtenay Youghal had openly proclaimed the fact as something unchallenged and understood matters seemed placed at once on a more advanced footing. The warm sunlit garden grew suddenly into a heaven that held the secret of eternal happiness. Youth and comeliness would always walk here, under the low-boughed mulberry trees, as unchanging as the leaden otter that for ever preyed on the leaden salmon on the edge of the old fountain, and somehow the lovers would always wear the aspect of herself and the boy who was talking to the four white swans by the water steps. Youghal was right; this was the real heaven of one's dreams and longings, immeasurably removed from that Rue de la Paix Paradise about which one professed utterly insincere hankerings in places of public worship. Elaine drank her tea in a happy silence;

besides being a brilliant talker Youghal understood the rarer art of being a non-talker on occasion.

Comus came back across the grass swinging the empty basket-dish in his hand.

'Swans were very pleased,' he cried gaily, 'and said they hoped I would keep the bread-and-butter dish as a souvenir of a happy tea-party. I may really have it, mayn't I?' he continued in an anxious voice; 'it will do to keep studs and things in. You don't want it.'

'It's got the family crest on it,' said Elaine. Some of the happiness had died out of her eyes.

'I'll have that scratched off and my own put on,' said Comus.

'It's been in the family for generations,' protested Elaine, who did not share Comus's view that because you were rich your lesser possessions could have no value in your eyes.

'I want it dreadfully,' said Comus sulkily, 'and you've heaps of other things to put bread-and-butter in.'

For the moment he was possessed by an overmastering desire to keep the dish at all costs; a look of greedy determination dominated his face, and he had not for an instant relaxed his grip of the coveted object.

Elaine was genuinely angry by this time, and was busily telling herself that it was absurd to be put out over such a trifle; at the same moment a sense of justice was telling her that Comus was displaying a good deal of rather shabby selfishness. And somehow her chief anxiety at the moment was to keep Courtenay Youghal from seeing that she was angry.

'I know you don't really want it, so I'm going to keep it,' persisted Comus.

'It's too hot to argue,' said Elaine.

'Happy mistress of your destinies,' laughed Youghal; 'you can suit your disputations to the desired time and temperature. I have to go and argue, or what is worse, listen to other people's arguments, in a hot and doctored atmosphere suitable to an invalid lizard.'

'You haven't got to argue about a bread-and-butter dish,' said Elaine.

'Chiefly about bread-and-butter,' said Youghal; 'our great preoccupation is other people's bread-and-butter. They earn or produce the material, but we busy ourselves with making rules how it shall be cut up, and the size of the slices, and how much butter shall go on how much bread. That is what is called legislation. If we could only make rules as to how the bread-and-butter should be digested we should be quite happy.'

Elaine had been brought up to regard Parliament as something to be treated with cheerful solemnity, like illness or family reunions. Youghal's flippant disparagement of the career in which he was involved did not, however, jar on her susceptibilities. She knew him to be not only a lively and effective debater but an industrious worker on committees. If he made light of his labours, at least he afforded no one else a loophole for doing so. And certainly the Parliamentary atmosphere was not uninviting on this hot afternoon.

'When must you go?' she asked sympathetically.

Youghal looked ruefully at his watch. Before he could answer, a cheerful hoot came through the air, as of an owl joyously challenging the sunlight with a foreboding of the coming night. He sprang laughing to his feet.

'Listen! My summons back to my galley,' he cried. 'The Gods have given me an hour in this enchanted garden, so I must not complain.'

Then in a lower voice he almost whispered, 'It's the Persian debate to-night.'

It was the one hint he had given in the midst of his talking and laughing that he was really keenly enthralled in the work that lay before him. It was the one little intimate touch that gave Elaine the knowledge that he cared for her opinion of his work.

Comus, who had emptied his cigarette-case, became suddenly clamorous at the prospect of being temporarily stranded without a smoke. Youghal took the last remaining cigarette from his own case and gravely bisected it.

'Friendship could go no farther,' he observed, as he gave one-half to the doubtfully appeased Comus, and lit the other himself.

'There are heaps more in the hall,' said Elaine.

'It was only done for the Saint Martin of Tours effect,' said Youghal; 'I hate smoking when I'm rushing through the air. Good-bye.'

57

The departing galley-slave stepped forth into the sunlight, radiant and confident. A few minutes later Elaine could see glimpses of his white car as it rushed past the rhododendron bushes. He woos best who leaves first, particularly if he goes forth to battle or the semblance of battle.

Somehow Elaine's garden of Eternal Youth had already become clouded in its imagery. The girl-figure who walked in it was still distinctly and unchangingly herself, but her companion was more blurred and undefined, as a picture that has been superimposed on another.

Youghal sped townward well satisfied with himself. To-morrow he reflected, Elaine would read his speech in her morning paper, and he knew in advance that it was not going to be one of his worst efforts. He knew almost exactly where the punctuations of laughter and applause would burst in, he knew that nimble fingers in the Press Gallery would be taking down each gibe and argument as he flung it at the impassive Minister confronting him, and that the fair lady of his desire would be able to judge what manner of young man this was who spent his afternoon in her garden, lazily chaffing himself and his world.

And he further reflected, with an amused chuckle, that she would be vividly reminded of Comus for days to come, when she took her afternoon tea, and saw the bread-and-butter reposing in an unaccustomed dish.

CHAPTER VII

TOWARDS four o'clock on a hot afternoon Francesca stepped out from a shop entrance near the Piccadilly end of Bond Street and ran almost into the arms of Merla Blathlington. The afternoon seemed to get instantly hotter. Merla was one of those human flies that buzz; in crowded streets, at bazaars and in warm weather, she attained to the proportions of a human bluebottle. Lady Caroline Benaresq had openly predicted that a special fly-paper was being reserved for her accommodation in another world; others, however, held the opinion that she would be miraculously multiplied in a future state, and that four or more Merla Blathlingtons, according to deserts, would be in perpetual and unremitting attendance on each lost soul.

'Here we are,' she cried, with a glad eager buzz, 'popping in and out of the shops like rabbits; not that rabbits do pop in and out of shops very extensively.'

It was evidently one of her bluebottle days.

'Don't you love Bond Street?' she gabbled on. 'There's something so unusual and distinctive about it; no other street anywhere else is quite like it. Don't you know those ikons and images and things scattered up and down Europe, that are supposed to have been painted or carved, as the case may be, by St Luke or Zaccheus, or somebody of that sort; I always like to think that some notable person of those times designed Bond Street. St Paul, perhaps. He travelled about a lot.'

'Not in Middlesex, though,' said Francesca.

'One can't be sure,' persisted Merla; 'when one wanders about as much as he did one gets mixed up and forgets where one *has* been. I can never remember whether I've been to the Tyrol twice and St Moritz once, or the other way about; I always have to ask my maid. And there's something about the name Bond that suggests St Paul; didn't he write a lot about the bond and the free?'

59

'I fancy he wrote in Hebrew or Greek,' objected Francesca; 'the word wouldn't have the least resemblance.'

'So dreadfully non-committal to go about pamphleteering in those bizarre languages,' complained Merla; 'that's what makes all those people so elusive. As soon as you try to pin them down to a definite statement about anything you're told that some vitally important word has fifteen other meanings in the original. I wonder our Cabinet Ministers and politicians don't adopt a sort of dog-Latin or Esperanto jargon to deliver their speeches in; what a lot of subsequent explaining away would be saved! But to go back to Bond Street—not that we've left it——'

'I'm afraid I must leave it now,' said Francesca, preparing to turn up Grafton Street. 'Good-bye.'

'Must you be going? Come and have tea somewhere. I know of a cosy little place where one can talk undisturbed.'

Francesca repressed a shudder and pleaded an urgent engagement.

'I know where you're going,' said Merla, with the resentful buzz of a bluebottle that finds itself thwarted by the cold unreasoning resistance of a windowpane. 'You're going to play bridge at Serena Golackly's. She never asks me to her bridge parties.'

Francesca shuddered openly this time; the prospect of having to play bridge anywhere in the near neighbourhood of Merla's voice was not one that could be contemplated with ordinary calmness.

'Good-bye,' she said again firmly, and passed out of earshot; it was rather like leaving the machinery section of an exhibition. Merla's diagnosis of her destination had been a correct one; Francesca made her way slowly through the hot streets in the direction of Serena Golackly's house on the far side of Berkeley Square. To the blessed certainty of finding a game of bridge, she hopefully added the possibility of hearing some fragments of news which might prove interesting and enlightening. And of enlightenment on a particular subject, in which she was acutely and personally interested, she stood in some need. Comus of late had been provokingly reticent as to his movements and doings; partly, perhaps, because it was his nature to be provoking, partly because the daily bickerings over money matters were gradually choking

other forms of conversation. Francesca had seen him once or twice in the Park in the desirable company of Elaine de Frey, and from time to time she heard of the young people as having danced together at various houses; on the other hand, she had seen and heard quite as much evidence to connect the heiress's name with that of Courtenay Youghal. Beyond this meagre and conflicting and altogether tantalizing information, her knowledge of the present position of affairs did not go. If either of the young men was seriously 'making the running', it was probable that she would hear some sly hint or open comment about it from one of Serena's gossip-laden friends, without having to go out of her way to introduce the subject and unduly disclose her own state of ignorance. And a game of bridge, played for moderately high points, gave ample excuse for convenient lapses into reticence; if questions took an embarrassingly inquisitive turn, one could always find refuge in a defensive spade.

The afternoon was too warm to make bridge a generally popular diversion, and Serena's party was a comparatively small one. Only one table was incomplete when Francesca made her appearance on the scene; at it was seated Serena herself, confronted by Ada Spelvexit, whom everyone was wont to explain as 'one of the Cheshire Spelvexits', as though any other variety would have been intolerable. Ada Spelvexit was one of those naturally stagnant souls who take infinite pleasure in what are called 'movements'. 'Most of the really great lessons I have learned have been taught me by the Poor', was one of her favourite statements. The one great lesson that the Poor in general would have liked to have taught her, that their kitchens and sickrooms were not unreservedly at her disposal as private lecture halls, she had never been able to assimilate. She was ready to give them unlimited advice as to how they should keep the wolf from their doors, but in return she claimed and enforced for herself the penetrating powers of an east wind or a dust-storm. Her visits among her wealthier acquaintances were equally extensive and enterprising, and hardly more welcome; in country-house parties, while partaking to the fullest extent of the hospitality offered her, she made a practice of unburdening herself of homilies on the evils of leisure and luxury, which did not particularly endear her to her fellow-guests.

Hostesses regarded her philosophically as a form of social measles which everyone had to have once.

The third prospective player, Francesca noted without any special enthusiasm, was Lady Caroline Benaresq. Lady Caroline was far from being a remarkably good bridge player, but she always managed to domineer mercilessly over any table that was favoured with her presence, and generally managed to win. A domineering player usually inflicts the chief damage and demoralization on his partner; Lady Caroline's special achievement was to harass and demoralize partner and opponents alike.

'Weak and weak,' she announced in her gentle voice, as she cut her hostess for a partner; 'I suppose we had better play only five shillings a hundred.'

Francesca wondered at the old woman's moderate assessment of the stake, knowing her fondness for highish play and her usual good luck in card holding.

'I don't mind what we play,' said Ada Spelvexit, with an incautious parade of elegant indifference; as a matter of fact she was inwardly relieved and rejoicing at the reasonable figure proposed by Lady Caroline, and she would certainly have demurred if a higher stake had been suggested. She was not as a rule a successful player, and money lost at cards was always a poignant bereavement to her.

'Then as you don't mind we'll make it ten shillings a hundred,' said Lady Caroline, with the pleased chuckle of one who has spread a net in the sight of a bird and disproved the vanity of the proceeding.

It proved a tiresome ding-dong rubber, with the strength of the cards slightly on Francesca's side, and the luck of the table going mostly the other way. She was too keen a player not to feel a certain absorption in the game once it had started, but she was conscious to-day of a distracting interest that competed with the momentary importance of leads and discards and declarations. The little accumulations of talk that were unpent during the dealing of the hands became as noteworthy to her alert attention as the play of the hands themselves.

'Yes, quite a small party this afternoon,' said Serena, in reply to a seemingly casual remark on Francesca's part; 'and two or three non-players, which is unusual on a Wednesday. Canon Besomley was here just before you came; you know, the big preaching man.'

'I've been to hear him scold the human race once or twice,' said Francesca.

'A strong man with a wonderfully strong message,' said Ada Spelvexit, in an impressive and assertive tone.

'The sort of popular pulpiteer who spanks the vices of his age and lunches with them afterwards,' said Lady Caroline.

'Hardly a fair summary of the man and his work,' protested Ada. 'I've been to hear him many times when I've been depressed or discouraged, and I simply can't tell you the impression his words leave——'

'At least you can tell us what you intend to make trumps,' broke in Lady Caroline gently.

'Diamonds,' pronounced Ada, after a rather flurried survey of her hand.

'Doubled,' said Lady Caroline, with increased gentleness, and a few minutes later she was pencilling an addition of twenty-four to her score.

'I stayed with his people down here in Herefordshire last May,' said Ada, returning to the unfinished theme of the Canon; 'such an exquisite rural retreat, and so restful and healing to the nerves. Real country scenery; apple blossom everywhere.'

'Surely only on the apple trees!' said Lady Caroline.

Ada Spelvexit gave up the attempts to reproduce the decorative setting of the Canon's home-life, and fell back on the small but practical consolation of scoring the odd trick on her opponent's declaration of hearts.

'If you had led your highest club to start with instead of the nine, we should have saved the trick,' remarked Lady Caroline to her partner in a tone of coldly gentle reproof; 'it's no use, my dear,' she continued, as Serena flustered out a halting apology, 'no earthly use to attempt to play bridge at one table and try to see and hear what's going on at two or three other tables.'

'I can generally manage to attend to more than one thing at a time,' said Serena rashly; 'I think I must have a sort of double brain.'

'Much better to economize and have one really good one,' observed Lady Caroline.

'*La belle dame sans merci* scoring a verbal trick or two as usual,' said a player at another table in a discreet undertone.

'Did I tell you Sir Edward Roan is coming to my next big evening?' said Serena hurriedly, by way, perhaps, of restoring herself a little in her own esteem.

'Poor dear good Sir Edward! What have you made trumps?' asked Lady Caroline, in one breath.

'Clubs,' said Francesca; 'and pray, why these adjectives of commiseration?'

Francesca was a Ministerialist by family interest and allegiance, and was inclined to take up the cudgels at the suggested disparagement aimed at the Foreign Secretary.

'He amuses me so much,' purred Lady Caroline. Her amusement was usually of the sort that a sporting cat derives from watching the Swedish exercises of a well-spent and carefully thought-out mouse.

'Really? He has been rather a brilliant success at the Foreign Office, you know,' said Francesca.

'He reminds one so of a circus elephant—infinitely more intelligent than the people who direct him, but quite content to go on putting his foot down or taking it up as may be required, quite unconcerned whether he steps on a meringue or a hornet's nest in the process of going where he's expected to go.'

'How can you say such things!' protested Francesca.

'I can't,' said Lady Caroline; 'Courtenay Youghal said it in the House last night. Didn't you read the debate? He was really rather in form. I disagree entirely with his point of view, of course, but some of the things he says have just enough truth behind them to redeem them from being merely smart; for instance, his summing up of the Government's attitude towards our embarrassing Colonial Empire in the wistful phrase "Happy is the country that has no geography". '

'What an absurdly unjust thing to say!' put in Francesca; 'I daresay some of our Party at some time have taken up that attitude, but every one knows that Sir Edward is a sound Imperialist at heart.'

'Most politicians are something or other at heart, but no one would be rash enough to insure a politican against heart failure. Particularly when he happens to be in office.'

'Anyhow, I don't see that the Opposition leaders would have acted any differently in the present case,' said Francesca.

'One should always speak guardedly of the Opposition leaders,' said Lady Caroline, in her gentlest voice; 'one never knows what a turn in the situation may do for them.'

'You mean they may one day be at the head of affairs?' asked Serena briskly.

'I mean they may one day lead the Opposition. One never knows.'

Lady Caroline had just remembered that her hostess was on the Opposition side in politics.

Francesca and her partner scored four tricks in clubs; the game stood irresolutely at twenty-four all.

'If you had followed the excellent lyrical advice given to the Maid of Athens and returned my heart we should have made two more tricks and gone game,' said Lady Caroline to her partner.

'Mr Youghal seems pushing himself to the fore of late,' remarked Francesca, as Serena took up the cards to deal. Since the young politician's name had been introduced into their conversation the opportunity for turning the talk more directly on him and his affairs was too good to be missed.

'I think he's got a career before him,' said Serena; 'the House always fills when he's speaking, and that's a good sign. And then he's young and got rather an attractive personality, which is always something in the political world.'

'His lack of money will handicap him, unless he can find himself a rich wife or persuade someone to die and leave him a fat legacy,' said Francesca; 'since M.P.s have become the recipients of a salary rather more is expected and demanded of them in the expenditure line than before.'

'Yes, the House of Commons still remains rather at the opposite pole of the Kingdom of Heaven as regards entrance qualifications,' observed Lady Caroline.

'There ought to be no difficulty about Youghal picking up a girl with money,' said Serena; 'with his prospects he would make an excellent husband for any woman with social ambitions.'

And she half sighed, as though she almost regretted that a previous matrimonial arrangement precluded her from entering into the competition on her own account.

Francesca, under an assumption of languid interest, was watching Lady Caroline narrowly for some hint of suppressed knowledge of Youghal's courtship of Miss de Frey.

'Whom are you marrying and giving in marriage?'

The question came from George St Michael, who had strayed over from a neighbouring table, attracted by the fragments of small-talk that had reached his ears.

St Michael was one of those dapper, bird-like illusorily-active men, who seem to have been in a certain stage of middle-age for as long as human memory can recall them. A close-cut peaked beard lent a certain dignity to his appearance—a loan which the rest of his features and mannerisms were continually and success-fully repudiating. His profession, if he had one, was submerged in his hobby, which consisted of being an advance-agent for small happenings or possible happenings that were or seemed imminent in the social world around him; he found a perpetual and unflagging satisfaction in acquiring and retailing any stray items of gossip or information, particularly of a matrimonial nature, that chanced to come his way. Given the bare outline of an officially announced engagement, he would immediately fill it in with all manner of details, true or, at any rate, probable, drawn from his own imagination or from some equally exclusive source. The *Morning Post* might content itself with the mere statement of the arrange-ment which would shortly take place, but it was St Michael's breathless little voice that proclaimed how the contracting parties had originally met over a salmon-fishing incident, why the Guards' Chapel would not be used, why her Aunt Mary had at first opposed the match, how the question of the children's religious upbringing had been compromised, etc., etc., to all whom it might interest and to many whom it might not. Beyond his industriously-earned pre-eminence in this special branch of intelligence, he was chiefly noteworthy for having a wife reputed to be the tallest and thinnest woman in the Home Counties. The two were sometimes seen together in Society, where they passed under the collective name of St Michael and All Angles.

'We were trying to find a rich wife for Courtenay Youghal,' said Serena, in answer to St Michael's question.

'Ah, there I'm afraid you're a little late,' he observed, glowing with the importance of pending revelation; 'I'm afraid you're a little late,' he repeated, watching the effect of his words as a gardener might watch the development of a bed of carefully tended asparagus. 'I think the young gentleman has been before you and already found himself a rich mate in prospect.'

He lowered his voice as he spoke, not with a view to imparting impressive mystery to his statement, but because there were other table groups within hearing to whom he hoped presently to have the privilege of re-disclosing his revelation.

'Do you mean——?' began Serena.

'Miss de Frey,' broke in St Michael hurriedly, fearful lest his revelation should be forestalled, even in guesswork; 'quite an ideal choice, the very wife for a man who means to make his mark in politics. Twenty-four thousand a year, with prospects of more to come, and a charming place of her own not too far from town. Quite the type of girl, too, who will make a good political hostess, brains without being brainy, you know. Just the right thing. Of course, it would be premature to make any definite announcement at present——'

'It would hardly be premature for my partner to announce what she means to make trumps,' interrupted Lady Caroline, in a voice of such sinister gentleness that St Michael fled headlong back to his own table.

'Oh, is it me? I beg your pardon. I leave it,' said Serena.

'Thank you. No trumps,' declared Lady Caroline. The hand was successful, and the rubber ultimately fell to her with a comfortable margin of honours. The same partners cut together again, and this time the cards went distinctly against Francesca and Ada Spelvexit, and a heavily piled-up score confronted them at the close of the rubber. Francesca was conscious that a certain amount of rather erratic play on her part had at least contributed to the result. St Michael's incursion into the conversation had proved rather a powerful distraction to her ordinarily sound bridge-craft.

Ada Spelvexit emptied her purse of several gold pieces, and infused a corresponding degree of superiority into her manner.

'I must be going now,' she announced; 'I'm dining early. I have to give an address to some charwomen afterwards.'

'Why?' asked Lady Caroline, with a disconcerting directness that was one of her most formidable characteristics.

'Oh, well, I have some things to say to them that I daresay they will like to hear,' said Ada, with a thin laugh.

Her statement was received with a silence that betokened profound unbelief in any such probability.

'I go about a good deal among working-class women,' she added.

'No one has ever said it,' observed Lady Caroline, 'but how painfully true it is that the poor have us always with them!'

Ada Spelvexit hastened her departure; the marred impressiveness of her retreat came as a culminating discomfiture on the top of her ill-fortune at the card-table. Possibly, however, the multiplication of her own annoyances enabled her to survey charwomen's troubles with increased cheerfulness. None of them, at any rate, had spent an afternoon with Lady Caroline.

Francesca cut in at another table, and with better fortune attending on her, succeeded in winning back most of her losses. A sense of satisfaction was distinctly dominant as she took leave of her hostess. St Michael's gossip, or rather the manner in which it had been received, had given her a clue to the real state of affairs, which, however slender and conjectural, at least pointed in the desired direction. At first she had been horribly afraid lest she should be listening to a definite announcement which would have been the death-blow to her hopes, but as the recitation went on without any of those assured little minor details which St Michael so loved to supply, she had come to the conclusion that it was merely a piece of intelligent guesswork. And if Lady Caroline had really believed in the story of Elaine de Frey's virtual engagement to Courtenay Youghal she would have taken a malicious pleasure in encouraging St Michael in his confidences, and in watching Francesca's discomfiture under the recital. The irritated manner in which she had cut short the discussion betrayed the fact that, as far as the old woman's information went, it was Comus, and not Courtenay Youghal, who held the field. And in this particular case Lady Caroline's information was likely to be nearer the truth than St Michael's confident gossip.

Francesca always gave a penny to the first crossing-sweeper or match-seller she chanced across after a successful sitting at bridge. This afternoon she had come out of the fray some fifteen shillings to the bad, but she gave two pennies to a crossing-sweeper at the north-west corner of Berkeley Square as a sort of thank-offering to the gods.

CHAPTER VIII

IT was a fresh rain-repentant afternoon, following a morning that had been sultry and torrentially wet by turns: the sort of afternoon that impels people to talk graciously of the rain as having done a lot of good, its chief merit in their eyes probably having been its recognition of the art of moderation. Also it was an afternoon that invited bodily activity after the convalescent languor of the earlier part of the day. Elaine had instinctively found her way into her riding-habit and sent an order down to the stables—a blessed oasis that still smelt sweetly of horse and hay and cleanliness in a world that reeked of petrol, and now she set her mare at a smart pace through a succession of long-stretching country lanes. She was due some time that afternoon at a garden-party, but she rode with determination in an opposite direction. In the first place, neither Comus nor Courtenay would be at the party, which fact seemed to remove any valid reason that could be thought of for inviting her attendance thereat; in the second place about a hundred human beings would be gathered there, and human gatherings were not her most crying need at the present moment. Since her last encounter with her wooers, under the cedars in her own garden, Elaine realized that she was either very happy or cruelly unhappy, she could not quite determine which. She seemed to have what she most wanted in the world lying at her feet, and she was dreadfully uncertain in her more reflective moments whether she really wanted to stretch out her hand and take it. In was all very like some situation in an *Arabian Nights* tale or a story of Pagan Hellas, and consequently the more puzzling and disconcerting to a girl brought up on the methodical lines of Victorian Christianity. Her appeal court was in permanent session these last few days, but it gave no decisions, at least none that she would listen to. And the ride on her fast light-stepping little mare, alone and unattended, through the fresh-smelling leafy lanes into unexplored country, seemed just what she wanted at the moment. The mare made some small delicate pretence of being road-shy, not the staring dolt-like kind of nervousness that shows itself in an irritating hanging-back as each conspicuous wayside object presents itself, but the nerve-flutter of an imaginative animal that merely results in a quick whisk of the head and a swifter bound forward. She might have paraphrased the mental attitude of the immortalized Peter Bell into

> *A basket underneath a tree*
> *A yellow tiger is to me,*
> *If it is nothing more.*

The more really alarming episodes of the road, the hoot and whir of a passing motor-car or the loud vibrating hum of a wayside threshing-machine, were treated with indifference.

On turning a corner out of a narrow coppice-bordered lane into a wider road that sloped steadily upward in a long stretch of hill, Elaine saw, coming toward her at no great distance, a string of yellow-painted vans, drawn for the most part by skewbald or speckled horses. A certain rakish air about these oncoming road-craft proclaimed them as belonging to a travelling wild-beast show, decked out in the rich primitive colouring that one's taste in childhood would have insisted on before it had been schooled in the artistic value of dullness. It was an unlooked-for and distinctly unwelcome encounter. The mare had already commenced a sixfold scrutiny with nostrils, eyes, and daintily-pricked ears; one ear made hurried little backward movements to hear what Elaine was saying about the eminent niceness and respectability of the approaching caravan, but even Elaine felt that she would be unable satisfactorily to explain the elephants and camels that could certainly form part of the procession. To turn back would seem rather craven, and the mare might take fright at the manœuvre and try to bolt; a gate standing ajar at the entrance to a farmyard lane provided a convenient way out of the difficulty.

As Elaine pushed her way through she became aware of a man standing just inside the lane, who made a movement forward to open the gate for her.

'Thank you. I'm just getting out of the way of a wild-beast show,' she explained; 'my mare is tolerant of motors and traction-engines, but I expect camels—hallo!' she broke off, recognizing the man as an old acquaintance, 'I heard you had taken rooms in a farm-house somewhere. Fancy meeting you in this way!'

In the not very distant days of her little-girlhood, Tom Keriway had been a man to be looked upon with a certain awe and envy; indeed the glamour of his roving career would have fired the imagination, and wistful desire to do likewise, of many young Englishmen. It seemed to be the grown-up realization of the games played in dark rooms in winter firelit evenings, and the dreams dreamed over favourite books of adventure. Making Vienna his headquarters, almost his home, he had rambled where he listed through the lands of the Near and Middle East as leisurely and thoroughly as tamer souls might explore Paris. He had wandered through Hungarian horse-fairs, hunted shy crafty beasts on lonely Balkan hillsides, dropped himself pebble-wise into the stagnant human pool of some Bulgarian monastery, threaded his way through the strange racial mosaic of Salonika, listened with amused politeness to the shallow ultra-modern opinions of a voluble editor or lawyer in some wayside Russian town, or learned wisdom from a chance tavern companion, one of the atoms of the busy ant-stream of men and merchandise that moves untiringly round the shores of the Black Sea. And far and wide as he might roam, he always managed to turn up at frequent intervals, at ball and supper and theatre, in the gay Hauptstadt of the Habsburgs, haunting his favourite cafés and wine-vaults, skimming through his favourite news-sheets, greeting old acquaintances and friends, from ambassadors down to cobblers in the social scale. He seldom talked of his travels, but it might be said that his travels talked of him; there was an air about him that a German diplomat once summed up in a phrase: 'a man that wolves have sniffed at.'

And then two things happened, which he had not mapped out in his route; a severe illness shook half the life and all the energy out of him, and a heavy money loss brought him almost to the door of destitution. With something, perhaps, of the impulse which drives a stricken animal away from its kind, Tom Keriway left the haunts where he had known so much happiness, and withdrew into the shelter of a secluded farm-house lodging; more than ever he became to Elaine a hearsay personality. And now the chance meeting with the caravan had flung her across the threshold of his retreat.

'What a charming little nook you've got hold of!' she exclaimed with instinctive politeness, and then looked searchingly round, and discovered that she had spoken the truth; it really was charming. The farm-house had that intensely English look that one seldom sees out of Normandy. Over the whole scene of rickyard, garden, outbuildings, horsepond and orchard, brooded that air which seems rightfully to belong to out-of-the-way farmyards, an air of wakeful dreaminess which suggests that here man and beast and bird have got up so early that the rest of the world has never caught them up and never will.

Elaine dismounted, and Keriway led the mare round to a little paddock by the side of a great grey barn. At the end of the lane they could see the show go past, a string of lumbering vans and great striding beasts that seemed to link the vast silences of the desert with the noises and sights and smells, the naphtha-flares and advertisement hoardings and trampled orange-peel, of an endless succession of towns.

'You had better let the caravan pass well on its way before you get on the road again,' said Keriway; 'the smell of the beasts may make your mare nervous and restive going home.'

Then he called to a boy, who was busy with a hoe among some defiantly prosperous weeds, to fetch the lady a glass of milk and a piece of currant loaf.

'I don't know when I've seen anything so utterly charming and peaceful,' said Elaine, propping herself on a seat that a pear-tree had obligingly designed in the fantastic curve of its trunk.

'Charming, certainly,' said Keriway, 'but too full of the stress of its own little life struggle to be peaceful. Since I have lived here I've learnt, what I've always suspected, that a country farm-house, set away in a world of its own, is one of the most wonderful studies of interwoven happenings and tragedies that can be imagined. It is like the old chronicles of medieval Europe in the days when there was a sort of ordered anarchy between feudal lords and overlords, and burg-grafs, and mitred abbots, and prince-bishops, robber barons and merchant guilds, and Electors and so forth, all striving and contending and counterplotting, and interfering with each other under some vague code of loosely-applied rules. Here one sees it reproduced under one's eyes, like a musty page of black-letter come to life. Look at one little section of it, the poultry-life on the farm. Villa poultry, dull egg-machines, with records kept of how many ounces of food they eat, and how many pennyworths of eggs they lay, give you no idea of the wonder-life of these farm-birds; their feuds and jealousies, and carefully maintained prerogatives, their unsparing tyrannies and persecutions, their calculated courage and bravado or sedulously hidden cowardice, it might all be some human chapter from the annals of the old Rhineland or medieval Italy. And then, outside their own bickering wars and hates, the grim enemies that come up against them from the woodlands; the hawk that dashes among the coops like a moss-trooper raiding the border, knowing well that a charge of shot may tear him to bits at any moment. And the stoat, a creeping slip of brown fur a few inches long, intently and unstayably out for blood. And the hunger-taught master of craft, the red fox, who has waited perhaps half the afternoon for his chance while the fowls were dusting themselves under the hedge, and just as they were turning supper-ward to the yard one has stopped a moment to give her feathers a final shake and found death springing upon her. Do you know,' he continued, as Elaine fed herself and the mare with the morsels of currant-loaf, 'I don't think any tragedy in literature that I have ever come across impressed me so much as the first one that I spelled out slowly for myself in words of three letters: the bad fox has got the red hen. There was something so dramatically complete about it; the badness of the fox, added to all the traditional guile of his race, seemed to heighten the horror of the hen's fate, and there was such a suggestion of masterful malice about the word "got". One felt that a countryside in arms would not get that hen away from the bad fox. They used to think me a slow dull reader for not getting on with my lesson, but I used to sit and picture to myself the red hen, with its wings beating helplessly, screeching in terrified protest, or perhaps, if he had got it by the neck, with beak wide agape and silent, and eyes staring, as it left the farmyard for ever. I have seen blood-spilling and down-crushings and abject defeat here and there in my time, but the red hen has remained in my mind as the type of helpless tragedy.' He was silent for a moment as if he were again musing over the three-letter drama that had so dwelt in his childhood's imagination.

'Tell me some of the things you have seen in your time,' was the request that was nearly on Elaine's lips, but she hastily checked herself and substituted another.

'Tell me more about the farm, please.'

And he told her of a whole world, or rather of several inter-mingled worlds, set apart in this sleepy hollow in the hills, of beast lore and wood lore and farm craft, at times touching almost the border of witchcraft—passing lightly here, not with the probing eagerness of those who know nothing, but with the averted glance of those who fear to see too much. He told her of those things that slept and those that prowled when the dusk fell, of strange hunting cats, of the yard swine and the stalled cattle, of the farm folk themselves, as curious and remote in their way, in their ideas and fears and wants and tragedies, as the brutes and feathered stock that they tended. It seemed to Elaine as if a musty store of old-world children's books had been fetched down from some cobwebbed lumber-room and brought to life. Sitting there in the little paddock, grown thickly with tall weeds and rank grasses, and shadowed by the weather-beaten old grey barn, listening to this chronicle of wonderful things, half fanciful, half very real, she could scarcely believe that a few miles away there was a garden-party in full swing, with smart frocks and smart conversation, fashionable refreshments and fashionable music, and a fevered undercurrent of social strivings and snubbings. Did Vienna and the Balkan Mountains and the Black Sea seem as remote and hard to believe in, she wondered, to the man sitting by her side, who had discovered or invented this wonderful fairyland? Was it a true and merciful arrangement of fate and life that the things of the moment thrust out the after-taste of the things that had been? Here was one who had held much that was priceless in the hollow of his hand and lost it all, and he was happy and absorbed and well content with the little wayside corner of the world into which he had crept. And Elaine, who held so many desirable things in the hollow of her hand, could not make up her mind to be even moderately happy. She did not even know whether to take this hero of her childhood down from his pedestal, or to place him on a higher one; on the whole she was inclined to resent rather than approve the idea that ill-health and misfortune could so completely subdue and tame an erstwhile bold and roving spirit.

The mare was showing signs of delicately-hinted impatience; the paddock, with its teasing insects and very indifferent grazing, had not thrust out the image of her own comfortable well-foddered loose-box. Elaine divested her habit of some remaining crumbs of bun-loaf and jumped lightly on to her saddle. As she rode slowly down the lane, with Keriway escorting her as far as its gate, she looked round at what had seemed to her, a short while ago, just a picturesque old farmstead, a place of bee-hives and hollyhocks and gabled cart-sheds; now it was in her eyes a magic city, with an undercurrent of reality beneath its magic.

'You are a person to be envied,' she said to Keriway; 'you have created a fairyland, and you are living in it yourself.'

'Envied?'

He shot the question out with sudden bitterness. She looked down and saw the wistful misery that had come into his face.

'Once,' he said to her, 'in a German paper I read a short story about a tame crippled crane that lived in the park of some small town. I forget what happened in the story, but there was one line that I shall always remember: "it was lame, that is why it was tame." '

He had created a fairyland, but assuredly he was not living in it.

CHAPTER IX

IN the warmth of a late June morning the long shaded stretch of raked earth, gravel-walk and rhododendron bush that is known affectionately as the Row was alive with the monotonous movement and alert stagnation appropriate to the time and place. The seekers after health, the seekers after notoriety and recognition, and the lovers of good exercise were all well represented on the galloping ground; the gravel-walk and chairs and long seats held a population whose varied instincts and motives would have baffled a social catalogue-maker. The children, handled or in perambulators, might be excused from instinct or motive; they were brought.

Pleasingly conspicuous among a bunch of indifferent riders pacing along by the rails where the onlookers were thickest was Courtenay Youghal, on his handsome plum-roan gelding Anne de Joyeuse. That delicately stepping animal had taken a prize at Islington and nearly taken the life of a stable-boy of whom he disapproved, but his strongest claims to distinction were his good looks and his high opinion of himself. Youghal evidently believed in thorough accord between horse and rider.

'Please stop and talk to me,' said a quiet beckoning voice from the other side of the rails, and Youghal drew rein and greeted Lady Veula Croot. Lady Veula had married into a family of commercial solidity and enterprising political nonentity. She had a devoted husband, some blonde teachable children, and a look of unutterable weariness in her eyes. To see her standing at the top of an expensively horticultured staircase receiving her husband's guests was rather like watching an animal performing on a music-hall stage. One always tells oneself that the animal likes it, and one always knows that it doesn't.

'Lady Veula is an ardent Free Trader, isn't she?' someone once remarked to Lady Caroline.

'I wonder,' said Lady Caroline, in her gently questioning voice; 'a woman whose dresses are made in Paris and whose marriage has

77

been made in heaven might be equally biased for and against free imports.'

Lady Veula looked at Youghal and his mount with slow critical appraisement, and there was a note of blended raillery and wistfulness in her voice.

'You two dear things, I should love to stroke you both, but I'm not sure how Joyeuse would take it. So I'll stroke you down verbally instead. I admired your attack on Sir Edward immensely, though of course I don't agree with a word of it. Your description of him building a hedge round the German cuckoo and hoping he was isolating it was rather sweet. Seriously though, I regard him as one of the pillars of the Administration.'

'So do I,' said Youghal; 'the misfortune is that he is merely propping up a canvas roof. It's just his regrettable solidity and integrity that makes him so expensively dangerous. The average Briton arrives at the same judgment about Roan's handling of foreign affairs as Omar does of the Supreme Being in his dealings with the world: "He's a good fellow and 'twill all be well." '

Lady Veula laughed lightly. 'My Party is in power, so I may exercise the privilege of being optimistic. Who is that who bowed to you?' she continued, as a dark young man with an inclination to stoutness passed by them on foot; 'I've seen him about a good deal lately. He's been to one or two of my dances.'

'Andrei Drakoloff,' said Youghal; 'he's just produced a play that has had a big success in Moscow and is certain to be extremely popular all over Russia. In the first three acts the heroine is supposed to be dying of consumption; in the last act they find she is really dying of cancer.'

'Are the Russians really such a gloomy people?'

'Gloom-loving, but not in the least gloomy. They merely take their sadness pleasurably, just as we are accused of taking our pleasures sadly. Have you noticed that dreadful Klopstock youth has been pounding past us at shortening intervals? He'll come up and talk if he catches your eye.'

'I only just know him. Isn't he at an agricultural college or something of the sort?'

'Yes, studying to be a gentleman farmer, he told me. I didn't ask if both subjects were compulsory.'

'You're really rather dreadful,' said Lady Veula, trying to look as if she thought so; 'remember, we are all equal in the sight of Heaven.'

For a preacher of wholesome truths her voice rather lacked conviction.

'If I and Ernest Klopstock are really equal in the sight of Heaven,' said Youghal, with intense complacency, 'I should recommend Heaven to consult an eye specialist.'

There was a heavy spattering of loose earth, and a squelching of saddle-leather, as the Klopstock youth lumbered up to the rails and delivered himself of loud, cheerful greetings. Joyeuse laid his ears well back as the ungainly bay cob and his appropriately matched rider drew up beside him; his verdict was reflected and endorsed by the cold stare of Youghal's eyes.

'I've been having a nailing fine time,' recounted the new-comer with clamorous enthusiasm; 'I was over in Paris last month and had lots of strawberries there, then I had a lot more in London, and now I've been having a late crop of them in Herefordshire, so I've quite a lot this year.' And he laughed as one who had deserved well and received well of Fate.

'The charm of that story,' said Youghal, 'is that it can be told in any drawing-room.' And with a sweep of his wide-brimmed hat to Lady Veula he turned the impatient Joyeuse into the moving stream of horses and horsemen.

'That woman reminds me of some verse I've read and liked,' thought Youghal, as Joyeuse sprang into a light showy canter that gave full recognition to the existence of observant human beings along the side-walk. 'Ah, I have it.'

And he quoted almost aloud, as one does in the exhilaration of a canter:

> 'How much I loved that way you had
> Of smiling most, when very sad,
> A smile which carried tender hints
> Of sun and spring,
> And yet, more than all other thing,
> Of weariness beyond all words.'

And having satisfactorily fitted Lady Veula on to a quotation he dismissed her from his mind. With the constancy of her sex she thought about him, his good looks and his youth and his railing tongue, till late in the afternoon.

While Youghal was putting Joyeuse through his paces under the elm trees of the Row a little drama in which he was directly interested was being played out not many hundred yards away. Elaine and Comus were indulging themselves in two pennyworths of Park chair, drawn aside just a little from the serried rows of sitters who were set out like bedded plants over an acre or so of turf. Comus was, for the moment, in a mood of pugnacious gaiety, disbursing a fund of pointed criticism and unsparing anecdote concerning those of the promenaders or loungers whom he knew personally or by sight. Elaine was rather quieter than usual, and the grave serenity of the Leonardo da Vinci portrait seemed intensified in her face this morning. In his leisurely courtship Comus had relied almost exclusively on his physical attraction and the fitful drollery of his wit and high spirits, and these graces had gone far to make him seem a very desirable and rather lovable thing in Elaine's eyes. But he had left out of account the disfavour which he constantly risked and sometimes incurred from his frank and undisguised indifference to other people's interests and wishes, including, at times, Elaine's. And the more that she felt that she liked him the more she was irritated by his lack of consideration for her. Without expecting that her every wish should become a law to him, she would at least have liked it to reach the formality of a Second Reading. Another important factor he had also left out of his reckoning, namely the presence on the scene of another suitor, who also had youth and wit to recommend him, and who certainly did not lack physical attractions. Comus, marching carelessly through unknown country to effect what seemed already an assured victory, made the mistake of disregarding the existence of an unbeaten army on his flank.

To-day Elaine felt that, without having actually quarrelled, she and Comus had drifted a little bit out of sympathy with one another. The fault she knew was scarcely hers, in fact from the most good-natured point of view it could hardly be denied that it was almost entirely his. The incident of the silver dish had lacked even the attraction of novelty; it had been one of a series, all bearing a

strong connecting likeness. There had been small unrepaid loans Elaine would not have grudged in themselves, though the application for them brought a certain qualm of distaste; with the perversity which seemed inseparable from his doings, Comus had always flung away a portion of his borrowings in some ostentatious piece of glaring and utterly profitless extravagance, which outraged all the canons of her upbringing without bringing him an atom of understandable satisfaction. Under these repeated discouragements it was not surprising that some small part of her affection should have slipped away, but she had come to the Park that morning with an unconfessed expectation of being gently wooed back to the mood of gracious forgetfulness that she was only too eager to assume. It was almost worth while being angry with Comus for the sake of experiencing the pleasure of being coaxed into friendliness again with the charm which he knew so well how to exert. It was delicious here under the trees on this perfect June morning, and Elaine had the blessed assurance that most of the women within range were envying her the companionship of the handsome merry-hearted youth who sat by her side. With special complacence she contemplated her cousin Suzette, who was self-consciously but not very elatedly basking in the attentions of her fiancé, an earnest-looking young man who was superintendent of a People's something-or-other on the south side of the river, and whose clothes Comus had described as having been made in Southwark rather than in anger.

Most of the pleasures in life must be paid for, and the chair-ticket vendor in due time made his appearance in quest of pennies. Comus paid him from out of a varied assortment of coins and then balanced the remainder in the palm of his hand. Elaine felt a sudden foreknowledge of something disagreeable about to happen, and a red spot deepened in her cheeks.

'Four shillings and fivepence and a halfpenny,' said Comus reflectively. 'It's a ridiculous sum to last me for the next three days, and I owe a card debt of over two pounds.'

'Yes?' commented Elaine dryly and with an apparent lack of interest in his exchequer statement. Surely, she was thinking hurriedly to herself, he could not be foolish enough to broach the matter of another loan.

'The card debt is rather a nuisance,' pursued Comus, with fatalistic persistency.

'You won seven pounds last week, didn't you?' asked Elaine; 'don't you put any of your winnings to balance losses?'

'The four shillings and the fivepence and the halfpenny represent the rearguard of the seven pounds,' said Comus; 'the rest have fallen by the way. If I can pay the two pounds to-day I daresay I shall win something more to go on with; I'm holding rather good cards just now. But if I can't pay it, of course I shan't show up at the club. So you see the fix I am in.'

Elaine took no notice of this indirect application. The Appeal Court was assembling in haste to consider new evidence, and this time there was the rapidity of sudden determination about its movement.

The conversation strayed away from the fateful topic for a few moments, and then Comus brought it deliberately back to the danger zone.

'It would be awfully nice if you would let me have a fiver for a few days, Elaine,' he said quickly; 'if you don't I really don't know what I shall do.'

'If you are really bothered about your card debt I will send you the two pounds by messenger boy early this afternoon.' She spoke quietly and with great decision. 'And I shall not be at the Connor's dance to-night,' she continued; 'it's too hot for dancing. I'm going home now; please don't bother to accompany me, I particularly wish to go alone.'

Comus saw that he had overstepped the mark of her good nature. Wisely he made no immediate attempt to force himself back into her good graces. He would wait till her indignation had cooled.

His tactics would have been excellent if he had not forgotten that unbeaten army on his flank.

Elaine de Frey had known very clearly what qualities she had wanted in Comus, and she had known, against all efforts at self-deception, that he fell far short of those qualities. She had been willing to lower her standard of moral requirements in proportion as she was fond of the boy, but there was a point beyond which she would not go. He had hurt her pride, besides alarming her sense of caution. Suzette, on whom she felt a thoroughly justified tendency to look down, had at any rate an attentive and considerate lover. Elaine walked towards the Park gates feeling that in one essential Suzette possessed something that had been denied to her, and at the gates she met Joyeuse and his spruce young rider preparing to turn homeward.

'Get rid of Joyeuse and come and take me out to lunch somewhere,' demanded Elaine.

'How jolly!' said Youghal. 'Let's go to the Corridor Restaurant. The head-waiter there is an old Viennese friend of mine and looks after me beautifully. I've never been there with a lady before, and he's sure to ask me afterwards in his fatherly way, if we're engaged.'

The lunch was a success in every way. There was just enough orchestral effort to immerse the conversation without drowning it, and Youghal was an attentive and inspired host. Through an open doorway Elaine could see the café reading-room, with its imposing array of *Neue Freie Presse*, *Berliner Tageblatt*, and other exotic newspapers hanging on the wall. She looked across at the young man seated opposite her, who gave one the impression of having centred the most serious efforts of his brain on his toilet and his food, and recalled some of the flattering remarks that the Press had bestowed on his recent speeches.

'Doesn't it make you conceited, Courtenay,' she asked, 'to look at all those foreign newspapers hanging there and know that most of them have got paragraphs and articles about your Persian speech?'

Youghal laughed.

'There's always a chastening corrective in the thought that some of them may have printed your portrait. When once you've seen your features hurriedly reproduced in the *Matin*, for instance, you feel you would like to be a veiled Turkish woman for the rest of your life.'

And Youghal gazed long and lovingly at his reflection in the nearest mirror, as an antidote against possible incitements to humility in the portrait gallery of fame.

Elaine felt a certain soothed satisfaction in the fact that this young man, whose knowledge of the Middle East was an embarrassment to Ministers at question time and in debate, was showing himself equally well informed on the subject of her culinary likes and dislikes. If Suzette could have been forced to attend as a witness at a neighbouring table she would have felt even happier.

'Did the head-waiter ask if we were engaged?' asked Elaine, when Courtenay had settled the bill, and she had finished collecting her sunshade and gloves and other impedimenta from the hands of obsequious attendants.

'Yes,' said Youghal, 'and he seemed quite crestfallen when I had to say "No". '

'It would be horrid to disappoint him when he's looked after us so charmingly,' said Elaine; 'tell him that we are.'

CHAPTER X

THE Rutland Galleries were crowded, especially in the neighbourhood of the tea-buffet, by a fashionable throng of art-patrons which had gathered to inspect Mervyn Quentock's collection of Society portraits. Quentock was a young artist whose abilities were just receiving due recognition from the critics; that the recognition was not overdue he owed largely to his perception of the fact that if one hides one's talent under a bushel one must be careful to point out to everyone the exact bushel under which it is hidden. There are two manners of receiving recognition: one is to be discovered so long after one's death that one's grandchildren have to write to the papers to establish their relationship; the other is to be discovered, like the infant Moses, at the very outset of one's career. Mervyn Quentock had chosen the latter and happier manner. In an age when many aspiring young men strive to advertise their wares by imparting to them a freakish imbecility, Quentock turned out work that was characterized by a pleasing delicate restraint, but he contrived to herald his output with a certain fanfare of personal eccentricity, thereby compelling an attention which might otherwise have strayed past his studio. In appearance he was the ordinary cleanly young Englishman, except, perhaps, that his eyes rather suggested a library edition of the *Arabian Nights*; his clothes matched his appearance and showed no taint of the sartorial disorder by which the bourgeois of the garden-city and the Latin Quarter anxiously seeks to proclaim his kinship with art and thought. His eccentricity took the form of flying in the face of some of the prevailing social currents of the day, but as a reactionary, never as a reformer. He produced a gasp of admiring astonishment in fashionable circles by refusing to paint actresses—except, of course, those who had left the legitimate drama to appear between the boards of Debrett. He absolutely declined to execute portraits of Americans unless they hailed from certain favoured States. His 'water-colour line', as a New York paper phrased it, earned for him a crop of angry criticism and a

85

shoal of Transatlantic commissions, and criticism and commissions were the things that Quentock most wanted.

'Of course he is perfectly right,' said Lady Caroline Benaresq, calmly rescuing a piled-up plate of caviare sandwiches from the neighbourhood of a trio of young ladies who had established themselves hopefully within easy reach of it. 'Art,' she continued, addressing herself to the Rev. Poltimore Vardon, 'has always been geographically exclusive. London may be more important from most points of view than Venice, but the art of portrait painting, which would never concern itself with a Lord Mayor, simply grovels at the feet of the Doges. As a Socialist I'm bound to recognize the right of Ealing to compare itself with Avignon, but one cannot expect the Muses to put the two on a level.'

'Exclusiveness,' said the Reverend Poltimore, 'has been the salvation of Art, just as the lack of it is proving the downfall of religion. My colleagues of the cloth go about zealously proclaiming the fact that Christianity, in some form or other, is attracting shoals of converts among all sorts of races and tribes that one had scarcely ever heard of, except in reviews of books of travel that one never read. That sort of thing was all very well when the world was more sparsely populated, but nowadays, when it simply teems with human beings, no one is particularly impressed by the fact that a few million, more or less, of converts, of a low stage of mental development, have accepted the teachings of some particular religion. It not only chills one's enthusiasm, it positively shakes one's convictions when one hears that the things one has been brought up to believe as true are being very favourably spoken of by Buriats and Samoyeds and Kanakas.'

The Rev. Poltimore Vardon had once seen a resemblance in himself to Voltaire, and had lived alongside the comparison ever since.

'No modern cult or fashion,' he continued, 'would be favourably influenced by considerations based on statistics; fancy adopting a certain style of hat or cut of coat, because it was being largely worn in Lancashire and the Midlands; fancy favouring a certain brand of champagne because it was being extensively patronized in German summer resorts! No wonder that religion is falling into disuse in this country under such ill-directed methods.'

86

'You can't prevent the heathen being converted if they choose to be,' said Lady Caroline; 'this is an age of toleration.'

'You could always deny it,' said Reverend Poltimore, 'like the Belgians do with regrettable occurrences in the Congo. But I would go further than that. I would stimulate the waning enthusiasm for Christianity in this country by labelling it as the exclusive possession of a privileged few. If one could induce the Duchess of Pelm, for instance, to assert that the Kingdom of Heaven, as far as the British Isles are concerned, is strictly limited to herself, two of the under-gardeners at Pelmby, and, possibly, but not certainly, the Dean of Dunster, there would be an instant reshaping of the popular attitude towards religious convictions and observances. Once let the idea get about that the Christian Church is rather more exclusive than the Lawn at Ascot, and you would have a quickening of religious life such as this generation has never witnessed. But as long as the clergy and the religious organizations advertise their creed on the lines of "Everybody ought to believe in us: millions do," one can expect nothing but indifference and waning faith.'

'Time is just as exclusive in its way as Art,' said Lady Caroline.

'In what way?' said the Reverend Poltimore.

'Your pleasantries about religion would have sounded quite clever and advanced in the early 'nineties. To-day they have a dreadfully warmed-up flavour. That is the great delusion of you would-be advanced satirists; you imagine you can sit down comfortably for a couple of decades saying daring and startling things about the age you live in, which, whatever other defects it may have, is certainly not standing still. The whole of the Sherard Blaw school of discursive drama suggests, to my mind, Early Victorian furniture in a travelling circus. However, you will always have relays of people from the suburbs to listen to the Mocking Bird of yesterday, and sincerely imagine it is the harbinger of something new and revolutionizing.'

'*Would* you mind passing that plate of sandwiches?' asked one of the trio of young ladies, emboldened by famine.

'With pleasure,' said Lady Caroline, deftly passing her a nearly empty plate of bread-and-butter.

'I meant the plate of caviare sandwiches. So sorry to trouble you,' persisted the young lady.

Her sorrow was misapplied; Lady Caroline had turned her attention to a new-comer.

'A very interesting exhibition,' Ada Spelvexit was saying; 'faultless technique, as far as I am a judge of technique, and quite a master-touch in the way of poses. But have you noticed how very animal his art is? He seems to shut out the soul from his portraits. I nearly cried when I saw dear Winifred depicted simply as a good-looking healthy blonde.'

'I wish you had,' said Lady Caroline; 'the spectacle of a strong, brave woman weeping at a private view in the Rutland Galleries would have been so sensational. It would certainly have been reproduced in the next Drury Lane drama. And I'm so unlucky; I never see these sensational events. I was ill with appendicitis, you know, when Lulu Braminguard dramatically forgave her husband, after seventeen years of estrangement, during a State luncheon party at Windsor. The old Queen was furious about it. She said it was so disrespectful to the cook to be thinking of such a thing at such a time.'

Lady Caroline's recollections of things that hadn't happened at the court of Queen Victoria were notoriously vivid; it was the very widespread fear that she might one day write a book of reminiscences that made her so universally respected.

'As for his full-length picture of Lady Brickfield,' continued Ada, ignoring Lady Caroline's commentary as far as possible, 'all the expression seems to have been deliberately concentrated in the feet; beautiful feet, no doubt, but still, hardly the most distinctive part of a human being.'

'To paint the right people at the wrong end may be an eccentricity, but it is scarcely an indiscretion,' pronounced Lady Caroline.

One of the portraits which attracted more than a passing flutter of attention was a costume study of Francesca Bassington. Francesca had secured some highly desirable patronage for the young artist, and in return he had enriched her pantheon of personal possessions with a clever piece of work into which he had thrown an unusual amount of imaginative detail. He had painted her in a costume of the Great Louis's brightest period, seated in front of a tapestry that was so prominent in the composition that it could scarcely be said to form part of the background. Flowers and fruit, in exotic profusion, were its dominant note; quinces, pomegranates, passion-flowers, giant convolvulus, great mauve-pink roses, and grapes that were already being pressed by gleeful cupids in a riotous Arcadian vintage, stood out on its woven texture. The same note was struck in the beflowered satin of the lady's kirtle, and in the pomegranate pattern of the brocade that draped the couch on which she was seated. The artist had called his picture 'Recolte'. And after one had taken in all the details of fruit and flower and foliage that earned the composition its name, one noted the landscape that showed through a broad casement in the left-hand corner. It was a landscape clutched in the grip of winter, naked, bleak, black-frozen; a winter in which things died and knew no rewakening. If the picture typified harvest, it was a harvest of artificial growth.

'It leaves a great deal to the imagination, doesn't it?' said Ada Spelvexit, who had edged away from the range of Lady Caroline's tongue.

'At any rate one can tell who it's meant for,' said Serena Golackly.

'Oh, yes, it's a good likeness of dear Francesca,' admitted Ada; 'of course, it flatters her.'

'That, too, is a fault on the right side in portrait painting,' said Serena; 'after all, if posterity is going to stare at one for centuries it's only kind and reasonable to be looking just a little better than one's best.'

'What a curiously unequal style the artist has!' continued Ada, almost as if she felt a personal grievance against him. 'I was just noticing what a lack of soul there was in most of his portraits. Dear Winifred, you know, who speaks so beautifully and feelingly at my gatherings for old women, he's made her look just an ordinary dairy-maidish blonde; and Francesca, who is quite the most soulless woman I've ever met, well, he's given her quite——'

'Hush!' said Serena, 'the Bassington boy is just behind you.'

Comus stood looking at the portrait of his mother with the feeling of one who comes suddenly across a once-familiar, half-forgotten acquaintance in unfamiliar surroundings. The likeness was undoubtedly a good one, but the artist had caught an expression in Francesca's eyes which few people had ever seen there. It was the expression of a woman who had forgotten for one short moment to be absorbed in the small cares and excitements of her life, the money worries and little social plannings, and had found time to send a look of half-wistful friendliness to some sympathetic companion. Comus could recall that look, fitful and fleeting, in his mother's eyes when she had been a few years younger, before her world had grown to be such a committee-room of ways and means. Almost as a re-discovery, he remembered that she had once figured in his boyish mind as a 'rather good sort', more ready to see the laughable side of a piece of mischief than to labour forth a reproof. That the bygone feeling of good-fellowship had been stamped out was, he knew, probably in great part his own doing, and it was possible that the old friendliness was still there under the surface of things, ready to show itself again if he willed it, and friends were becoming scarcer with him than enemies in these days. Looking at the picture with its wistful hint of a long-ago comradeship, Comus made up his mind that he very much wanted things to be back on their earlier footing, and to see again on his mother's face the look that the artist had caught and perpetuated in its momentary flitting. If the projected Elaine marriage came off, and in spite of recent maladroit behaviour on his part he still counted it an assured thing, much of the immediate cause for estrangement between himself and his mother would be removed, or at any rate easily removable. With the influence of Elaine's money behind him, he promised himself that he would find some occupation that would remove from himself the reproach of being a waster and idler. There were lots of careers, he told himself, that were open to a man with solid financial backing and good connections. There might yet be jolly times ahead, in which his mother would have her share of the good things that were going, and carking thin-lipped Henry Greech and other of Comus's detractors could take their sour looks and words out of sight and hearing. Thus, staring at the picture as though he were studying its every detail, and seeing really only that wistful friendly smile, Comus made his plans and dispositions for a battle that was already fought and lost.

The crowd grew thicker in the galleries, cheerfully enduring an amount of overcrowding that would have been fiercely resented in a railway carriage. Near the entrance Mervyn Quentock was talking to a Serene Highness, a lady who led a life of obtrusive usefulness, largely imposed on her by a good-natured inability to say 'No'. 'That woman creates a positive draught with the number of bazaars she opens,' a frivolously-spoken ex-Cabinet Minister had once remarked. At the present moment she was being whimsically apologetic.

'When I think of the legions of well-meaning young men and women to whom I've given away prizes for proficiency in art-school curriculum, I feel that I ought not to show my face inside a picture gallery. I always imagine that my punishment in another world will be perpetually sharpening pencils and cleaning palettes for unending relays of misguided young people whom I deliberately encouraged in their artistic delusions.'

'Do you suppose we shall all get appropriate punishments in another world for our sins in this?' asked Quentock.

'Not so much for our sins as for our indiscretions; they are the things which do the most harm and cause the greatest trouble. I feel certain that Christopher Columbus will undergo the endless torment of being discovered by parties of American tourists. You see I am quite old-fashioned in my ideas about the terrors and inconveniences of the next world. And now I must be running away; I've got to open a Free Library somewhere. You know the sort of thing that happens—one unveils a bust of Carlyle and makes a speech about Ruskin, and then people come in their thousands and read *Rabid Ralph, or Should He Have Bitten Her?* Don't forget, please, I'm going to have the medallion with the fat cupid sitting on a sundial. And just one thing more—perhaps I ought not to ask you, but you have such nice kind eyes, you embolden one to make daring requests, *would* you send me the recipe for those lovely chestnut-and-chicken-liver sandwiches? I know the ingredients, of course, but it's the proportions that make such a difference—just how much liver to how much chestnut, and what amount of red pepper and other things. Thank you so much. I really am going now.'

Staring round with a vague half-smile at everybody within nodding distance, Her Serene Highness made one of her characteristic exits, which Lady Caroline declared always reminded her of a scrambled egg slipping off a piece of toast. At the entrance she stopped for a moment to exchange a word or two with a young man who had just arrived. From a corner where he was momentarily hemmed in by a group of tea-consuming dowagers, Comus recognized the newcomer as Courtenay Youghal, and began slowly to labour his way towards him. Youghal was not at the moment the person whose society he most craved for in the world, but there was at least the possibility that he might provide an opportunity for a game of bridge, which was the dominant desire of the moment. The young politician was already surrounded by a group of friends and acquaintances, and was evidently being made the recipient of a salvo of congratulation—presumably on his recent performances in the Foreign Office debate, Comus concluded. But Youghal himself seemed to be announcing the event with which the congratulations were connected. Had some dramatic catastrophe overtaken the Government? Comus wondered. And then, as he pressed nearer, a chance word, the coupling of two names, told him the news.

CHAPTER XI

AFTER the momentous lunch at the Corridor Restaurant, Elaine had returned to Manchester Square (where she was staying with one of her numerous aunts) in a frame of mind that embraced a tangle of competing emotions. In the first place she was conscious of a dominant feeling of relief; in a moment of impetuosity, not wholly uninfluenced by pique, she had settled the problem which hours of hard thinking and serious heart-searching had brought no nearer to solution, and, although she felt just a little inclined to be scared at the headlong manner of her final decision, she had now very little doubt in her own mind that the decision had been the right one. In fact, the wonder seemed rather that she should have been so long in doubt as to which of her wooers really enjoyed her honest approval. She had been in love these many weeks past with an imaginary Comus, but now that she had definitely walked out of her dreamland she saw that nearly all the qualities that had appealed to her on his behalf had been absent from, or only fitfully present in, the character of the real Comus. And now that she had installed Youghal in the first place of her affections he had rapidly acquired in her eyes some of the qualities which ranked highest in her estimation. Like the proverbial buyer she had the happy feminine tendency of magnifying the worth of her possession as soon as she had acquired it. And Courtenay Youghal gave Elaine some justification for her sense of having chosen wisely. Above all other things, selfish and cynical though he might appear at times, he was unfailingly courteous and considerate towards her. That was a circumstance which would always have carried weight with her in judging any man; in this case its value was enormously heightened by contrast with the behaviour of her other wooer. And Youghal had in her eyes the advantage which the glamour of combat, even the combat of words and wire-pulling, throws over the fighter. He stood well in the forefront of a battle which however carefully stage-managed, however honeycombed with personal insincerities and overlaid with calculated mock-heroics, really meant something, really counted for good or wrong in the nation's development and the world's history. Shrewd parliamentary observers might have warned her that Youghal would never stand much higher in the political world than he did at present, as a brilliant Opposition free-lance, leading lively and rather meaningless forays against the dull and rather purposeless foreign policy of a Government that was scarcely either to be blamed for or congratulated on its handling of foreign affairs. The young politician had not the strength of character or convictions that keeps a man naturally in the forefront of affairs and gives his counsels a sterling value, and on the other hand his insincerity was not deep enough to allow him to pose artificially and successfully as a leader of men and shaper of movements. For the moment, however, his place in public life was sufficiently marked out to give him a secure footing in that world where people are counted individually and not in herds. The woman whom he would make his wife would have the chance, too, if she had the will and the skill, to become an individual who counted.

There was balm to Elaine in this reflection, yet it did not wholly suffice to drive out the feeling of pique which Comus had called into being by his slighting view of her as a convenient cash supply in moments of emergency. She found a certain satisfaction in scrupulously observing her promise, made earlier on that eventful day, and sent off a messenger with the stipulated loan. Then a reaction of compunction set in, and she reminded herself that in fairness she ought to write and tell her news in as friendly a fashion as possible to her dismissed suitor before it burst upon him from some other quarter. They parted on more or less quarrelling terms, it was true, but neither of them had foreseen the finality of the parting nor the permanence of the breach between them; Comus might even now be thinking himself half-forgiven, and the awakening would be rather cruel. The letter, however, did not prove an easy one to write; not only did it present difficulties of its own, but it suffered from the competing urgency of a desire to be doing something far pleasanter than writing explanatory and valedictory phrases. Elaine was possessed with an unusual but quite overmastering hankering to visit her cousin

94

Suzette Brankley. They met but rarely at each other's houses and very seldom anywhere else, and Elaine for her part was never conscious of feeling that their opportunities for intercourse lacked anything in the way of adequacy. Suzette accorded her just that touch of patronage which a moderately well-off and immoderately dull girl will usually try to mete out to an acquaintance who is known to be wealthy and suspected of possessing brains. In return Elaine armed herself with that particular brand of mock humility which can be so terribly disconcerting if properly wielded. No quarrel of any description stood between them and one could not legitimately have described them as enemies, but they never disarmed in one another's presence. A misfortune of any magnitude falling on one of them would have been sincerely regretted by the other, but any minor discomfiture would have produced a feeling very much akin to satisfaction. Human nature knows millions of these inconsequent little feuds, springing up and flourishing apart from any basis of racial, political, religious or economic causes, as a hint perhaps to crass unseeing altruists that enmity has its place and purpose in the world as well as benevolence.

Elaine had not personally congratulated Suzette since the formal announcement of her engagement to the young man with the dissentient tailoring effects. The impulse to go and do so now over-mastered her sense of what was due to Comus in the way of explanation. The letter was still in its blank unwritten stage, an unmarshalled sequence of sentences forming in her brain, when she ordered her car and made a hurried but well-thought-out change into her most sumptuously sober afternoon toilette. Suzette, she felt tolerably sure, would still be in the costume that she had worn in the Park that morning, a costume that aimed at elaboration of detail, and was damned with overmuch success.

Suzette's mother welcomed her unexpected visitor with obvious satisfaction. Her daughter's engagement, she explained, was not so brilliant from the social point of view as a girl of Suzette's attractions and advantages might have legitimately aspired to, but Egbert was a thoroughly commendable and dependable young man, who would very probably win his way before long to membership of the County Council.

'From there, of course, the road would be open to him to higher things.'

'Yes,' said Elaine, 'he might become an alderman.'

'Have you seen their photographs, taken together?' asked Mrs Brankley, abandoning the subject of Egbert's prospective career.

'No; do show me,' said Elaine, with a flattering show of interest; 'I've never seen that sort of thing before. It used to be the fashion once for engaged couples to be photographed together, didn't it?'

'It's very much the fashion now,' said Mrs Brankley assertively, but some of the complacency had filtered out of her voice.

Suzette came into the room, wearing the dress that she had worn in the Park that morning.

'Of course, you've been hearing all about *the* engagement from mother,' she cried, and then set to work conscientiously to cover the same ground.

'We met at Grindelwald, you know. He always calls me his Ice Maiden because we first got to know each other on the skating-rink. Quite romantic, wasn't it? Then we asked him to tea one day, and we got to be quite friendly. Then he proposed.'

'He wasn't the only one who was smitten with Suzette,' Mrs Brankley hastened to put in, fearful lest Elaine might suppose that Egbert had had things all his own way. 'There was an American millionaire who was quite taken with her, and a Polish count of a very old family. I assure you I felt quite nervous at some of our tea-parties.'

Mrs Brankley had given Grindelwald a sinister but rather alluring reputation among a large circle of untravelled friends as a place where the insolence of birth and wealth was held in precarious check from breaking forth into scenes of savage violence.

'My marriage with Egbert will, of course, enlarge the sphere of my life enormously,' pursued Suzette.

'Yes,' said Elaine; her eyes were rather remorselessly taking in the details of her cousin's toilette. It is said that nothing is sadder than victory except defeat. Suzette began to feel that the tragedy of both was concentrated in the creation which had given her such unalloyed gratification till Elaine had come on the scene.

'A woman can be so immensely helpful in the social way to a man who is making a career for himself. And I'm so glad to find that we've a great many ideas in common. We each made out a list of our idea of the hundred best books, and quite a number of them were the same.'

'He looks bookish,' said Elaine, with a critical glance at the photograph.

'Oh, he's not at all a bookworm,' said Suzette quickly, 'though he's tremendously well-read. He's quite the man of action.'

'Does he hunt?' asked Elaine.

'No, he doesn't get much time or opportunity for riding.'

'What a pity!' commented Elaine. 'I don't think I could marry a man who wasn't fond of riding.'

'Of course that's a matter of taste,' said Suzette stiffly; 'horsey men are not usually gifted with overmuch brains, are they?'

'There is as much difference between a horseman and a horsey man as there is between a well-dressed man and a dressy one,' said Elaine judicially; 'and you may have noticed how seldom a dressy woman really knows how to dress. As an old lady of my acquaintance observed the other day, some people are born with a sense of how to clothe themselves, others acquire it, others look as if their clothes had been thrust upon them.'

She gave Lady Caroline her due quotation marks, but the sudden tactfulness with which she looked away from her cousin's frock was entirely her own idea.

A young man entering the room at this moment caused a diversion that was rather welcome to Suzette.

'Here comes Egbert,' she announced, with an air of subdued triumph; it was at least a satisfaction to be able to produce the captive of her charms, alive and in good condition, on the scene. Elaine might be as critical as she pleased, but a live lover outweighed any number of well-dressed straight-riding cavaliers who existed only as a distant vision of the delectable husband.

Egbert was one of those men who have no small talk, but possess an inexhaustible supply of the larger variety. In whatever society he happened to be, and particularly in the immediate neighbourhood of an afternoon-tea table, with a limited audience of womenfolk, he gave the impression of someone who was addressing a public meeting, and would be happy to answer questions afterwards. A suggestion of gaslit mission-halls, wet umbrellas, and discreet applause seemed to accompany him everywhere. He was an exponent, among other things, of what he called New Thought, which seemed to lend itself conveniently to the employment of a good deal of rather stale phraseology. Probably in the course of some thirty odd years of existence he had never been of any notable use to man, woman, child, or animal, but it was his firmly-announced intention to leave the world a better, happier, purer place than he had found it; against the danger of any relapse to earlier conditions after his disappearance from the scene, he was, of course, powerless to guard. 'Tis not in mortals to ensure succession, and Egbert was admittedly mortal.

Elaine found him immensely entertaining, and would certainly have exerted herself to draw him out if such a proceeding had been at all necessary. She listened to his conversation with the complacent appreciation that one bestows on a stage tragedy, from whose calamities one can escape at any moment by the simple process of leaving one's seat. When at last he checked the flow of his opinions by a hurried reference to his watch, and declared that he must be moving on elsewhere, Elaine almost expected a vote of thanks to be accorded him, or to be asked to signify herself in favour of some resolution by holding up her hand.

When the young man had bidden the company a rapid business-like farewell, tempered in Suzette's case by the exact degree of tender intimacy that it would have been considered improper to omit or overstep, Elaine turned to her expectant cousin with an air of cordial congratulation.

'He is exactly the husband I should have chosen for you, Suzette.'

For the second time that afternoon Suzette felt a sense of waning enthusiasm for one of her possessions.

Mrs Brankley detected the note of ironical congratulation in her visitor's verdict.

'I suppose she means he's not her idea of a husband, but he's good enough for Suzette,' she observed to herself, with a snort that expressed itself somewhere in the nostrils of the brain. Then with a smiling air of heavy patronage she delivered herself of her one idea of a damaging counterstroke.

'And when are we to hear of your engagement, my dear?'

'Now,' said Elaine quietly, but with electrical effect; 'I came to announce it to you but I wanted to hear all about Suzette first. It will be formally announced in the papers in a day or two.'

'But who is it? Is it the young man who was with you in the Park this morning?' asked Suzette.

'Let me see, who was I with in the Park this morning? A very good-looking dark boy? Oh no, not Comus Bassington. Someone you know by name, anyway, and I expect you've seen his portrait in the papers.'

'A flying-man?' asked Mrs Brankley.

'Courtenay Youghal,' said Elaine.

Mrs Brankley and Suzette had often rehearsed in the privacy of their minds the occasion when Elaine should come to pay her personal congratulations to her engaged cousin. It had never been in the least like this.

On her return from her enjoyable afternoon visit Elaine found an express messenger letter waiting for her. It was from Comus, thanking her for her loan—and returning it.

'I suppose I ought never to have asked you for it,' he wrote, 'but you are always so deliciously solemn about money matters that I couldn't resist. Just heard the news of your engagement to Courtenay. Congrats. to you both. I'm far too stony broke to buy you a wedding present so I'm going to give you back the bread-and-butter dish. Luckily it still has your crest on it. I shall love to think of you and Courtenay eating bread-and-butter out of it for the rest of your lives.'

That was all he had to say on the matter about which Elaine had been preparing to write a long and kindly-expressed letter, closing a rather momentous chapter in her life and his. There was not a trace of regret or upbraiding in his note; he had walked out of their mutual fairyland as abruptly as she had, and to all appearances far more unconcernedly. Reading the letter again and again, Elaine could come to no decision as to whether this was merely a courageous gibe at defeat, or whether it represented the real value that Comus set on the thing that he had lost.

And she would never know. If Comus possessed one useless gift to perfection it was the gift of laughing at Fate even when it had struck him hardest. One day, perhaps, the laughter and mockery would be silent on his lips, and Fate would have the advantage of laughing last.

CHAPTER XII

A DOOR closed and Francesca Bassington sat alone in her well-beloved drawing-room. The visitor who had been enjoying the hospitality of her afternoon-tea table had just taken his departure. The *tête-à-tête* had not been a pleasant one, at any rate as far as Francesca was concerned, but at least it had brought her the information for which she had been seeking. Her *rôle* of looker-on from a tactful distance had necessarily left her much in the dark concerning the progress of the all-important wooing, but during the last few hours she had, on slender though significant evidence, exchanged her complacent expectancy for a conviction that something had gone wrong. She had spent the previous evening at her brother's house, and had naturally seen nothing of Comus in that uncongenial quarter; neither had he put in an appearance at the breakfast table the following morning. She had met him in the hall at eleven o'clock, and he had hurried past her, merely imparting the information that he would not be in till dinner that evening. He spoke in his sulkiest tone, and his face wore a look of defeat, thinly masked by an air of defiance; it was not the defiance of a man who is losing, but of one who has already lost.

Francesca's conviction that things had gone wrong between Comus and Elaine de Frey grew in strength as the day wore on. She lunched at a friend's house, but it was not a quarter where special social information of any importance was likely to come early to hand. Instead of the news she was hankering for, she had to listen to trivial gossip and speculation on the flirtations and 'cases' and 'affairs' of a string of acquaintances whose matrimonial projects interested her about as much as the nesting arrangements of the wildfowl in St James's Park.

'Of course,' said her hostess, with the duly impressive emphasis of a privileged chronicler, 'we've always regarded Claire as the marrying one of the family, so when Emily came to us and said, "I've got some news for you," we all said, "Claire's engaged!"

"Oh, no," said Emily, "it's not Claire this time, it's me." So then we had to guess who the lucky man was. "It can't be Captain Parminter," we all said, "because he's always been sweet on Joan." And then Emily said——'

The recording voice reeled off the catalogue of inane remarks with a comfortable purring complacency that held out no hope of an early abandoning of the topic. Francesca sat and wondered why the innocent acceptance of a cutlet and a glass of indifferent claret should lay one open to such unsparing punishment.

A stroll homeward through the Park after lunch brought no further enlightenment on the subject that was uppermost in her mind; what was worse, it brought her, without possibility of escape, within hailing distance of Merla Blathington, who fastened on to her with the enthusiasm of a lonely tsetse fly encountering an outpost of civilization.

'Just think,' she buzzed inconsequently, 'my sister in Cambridgeshire has hatched out thirty-three White Orpington chickens in her incubator!'

'What eggs did she put in it?' asked Francesca.

'Oh, some very special strain of White Orpington.'

'Then I don't see anything remarkable in the result. If she had put in crocodile's eggs and hatched out White Orpingtons, there might have been something to write to *Country Life* about.'

'What funny fascinating things these little green park-chairs are,' said Merla, starting off on a fresh topic; 'they always look so quaint and knowing when they're stuck away in pairs by themselves under the trees, as if they were having a heart-to-heart talk or discussing a piece of very private scandal. If they could only speak, what tragedies and comedies they could tell us of, what flirtations and proposals!'

'Let us be devoutly thankful that they can't,' said Francesca, with a shuddering recollection of the luncheon-table conversation.

'Of course, it would make one very careful what one said before them—or above them rather,' Merla rattled on, and then, to Francesca's infinite relief, she espied another acquaintance sitting in unprotected solitude, who promised to supply a more durable audience than her present rapidly moving companion. Francesca was free to return to her drawing-room in Blue Street to await with such patience as she could command the coming of some visitor who might be able to throw light on the subject that was puzzling and disquieting her. The arrival of George St Michael boded bad news, but at any rate news, and she gave him an almost cordial welcome.

'Well, you see I wasn't far wrong about Miss de Frey and Courtenay Youghal, was I?' he chirruped, almost before he had seated himself. Francesca was to be spared any further spinning-out of her period of uncertainty. 'Yes, it's officially given out,' he went on, 'and it's to appear in the *Morning Post* to-morrow. I heard it from Colonel Deel this morning, and he had it direct from Youghal himself. Yes, please, one lump; I'm not fashionable, you see.' He had made the same remark about the sugar in his tea with unfailing regularity for at least thirty years. Fashions in sugar are apparently stationary. 'They say,' he continued hurriedly, 'that he proposed to her on the Terrace of the House, and a division bell rang and he had to hurry off before she had time to give her answer, and when he got back she simply said, "The Ayes have it".' St Michael paused in his narrative to give an appreciative giggle.

'Just the sort of inanity that would go the rounds,' remarked Francesca, with the satisfaction of knowing that she was making the criticism direct to the author and begetter of the inanity in question. Now that the blow had fallen and she knew the full extent of its weight, her feeling towards the bringer of bad news, who sat complacently nibbling at her tea-cakes and scattering crumbs of tiresome small-talk at her feet, was one of whole-hearted dislike. She could sympathize with, or at any rate understand, the tendency of Oriental despots to inflict death or ignominious chastisement on messengers bearing tidings of misfortune and defeat, and St Michael, she perfectly well knew, was thoroughly aware of the fact that her hopes and wishes had been centred on the possibility of having Elaine for a daughter-in-law; every purring remark that his mean little soul prompted him to contribute to the conversation had an easily recognizable under-current of malice. Fortunately for her powers of polite endurance, which had been put to such searching and repeated tests that day, St Michael had planned out for himself a busy little time-table of afternoon visits, at each of which his self-appointed task of forestalling and embellishing the newspaper announcements of the Youghal–de Frey engagement would be hurriedly but thoroughly performed.

'They'll be quite one of the best-looking and most interesting couples of the season, won't they?' he cried, by way of farewell. The door closed, and Francesca Bassington sat alone in her drawing-room.

Before she could give way to the bitter luxury of reflection on the downfall of her hopes, it was prudent to take precautionary measures against unwelcome intrusion. Summoning the maid who had just speeded the departing St Michael, she gave the order: 'I am not at home this afternoon to Lady Caroline Benaresq.' On second thoughts she extended the taboo to all possible callers, and sent a telephone message to catch Comus at his club, asking him to come and see her as soon as he could manage before it was time to dress for dinner. Then she sat down to think, and her thinking was beyond the relief of tears.

She had built herself a castle of hopes, and it had not been a castle in Spain, but a structure well on the probable side of the Pyrenees. There had been a solid foundation on which to build. Miss de Frey's fortune was an assured and unhampered one, her liking for Comus had been an obvious fact; his courtship of her a serious reality. The young people had been much together in public, and their names had naturally been coupled in the matchmaking gossip of the day. The only serious shadow cast over the scene had been the persistent presence, in foreground or background, of Courtenay Youghal. And now the shadow suddenly stood forth as the reality, and the castle of hopes was a ruin, a hideous mortification of dust and débris, with the skeleton outlines of its chambers still standing to make mockery of its discomfited architect. The daily anxiety about Comus and his extravagant ways and intractable disposition had been gradually lulled by the prospect of his making an advantageous marriage, which would have transformed him from a ne'er-do-well and adventurer into a wealthy idler. He might even have been moulded, by the resourceful influence of an ambitious wife, into a man with some definite purpose in life. The prospect had vanished with cruel suddenness, and the anxieties were crowding back again, more insistent than ever. The boy had had his one good chance in the matrimonial market and missed it; if he were to transfer his attentions to some other well-dowered girl he would be marked down at once as a fortune-hunter, and that would constitute a heavy handicap to the most plausible of wooers. His liking for Elaine had evidently been genuine in its way, though perhaps it would have been rash to read any deeper sentiment into it, but even with the spur of his own inclination to assist him he had failed to win the prize that had seemed so temptingly within his reach. And in the dashing of his prospects, Francesca saw the threatening of her own. The old anxiety as to her precarious tenure of her present quarters put on again all its familiar terrors. One day, she foresaw, in the horribly near future, George St Michael would come pattering up her stairs with the breathless intelligence that Emmeline Chetrof was going to marry somebody or other in the Guards or the Record Office, as the case might be, and then there would be an uprooting of her life from its home and haven in Blue Street and a wandering forth to some cheap unhappy far-off dwelling, where the stately Van der Meulen and its companion host of beautiful and desirable things would be stuffed and stowed away in soulless surroundings, like courtly *émigrés* fallen on evil days. It was unthinkable, but the trouble was that it had to be thought about. And if Comus had played his cards well and transformed himself from an encumbrance into a son with wealth at his command, the tragedy which she saw looming in front of her might have been avoided, or at the worst whittled down to easily bearable proportions. With money behind one, the problem of where to live approaches more nearly to the simple question of where do you wish to live, and a rich daughter-in-law would have surely seen to it that she did not have to leave her square mile of Mecca and go out into the wilderness of bricks and mortar. If the house in Blue Street could not have been compounded for there were other desirable residences which would have been capable of consoling Francesca for her lost Eden. And now the detested Courtenay Youghal, with his mocking eyes and air of youthful cynicism, had stepped in and overthrown those golden hopes and plans whose non-fulfilment would make such a world of change in her future. Assuredly she had reason to feel bitter against that young man, and she was not disposed to take a very lenient view of Comus's own mismanagement of the affair; her greeting when he at last arrived was not couched in a sympathetic strain.

'So you have lost your chance with the heiress,' she remarked abruptly.

'Yes,' said Comus coolly; 'Courtenay Youghal has added her to his other successes.'

'And you have added her to your other failures,' pursued Francesca relentlessly; her temper had been tried that day beyond ordinary limits.

'I thought you seemed getting along so well with her,' she continued, as Comus remained uncommunicative.

'We hit it off rather well together,' said Comus, and added with deliberate bluntness, 'I suppose she got rather sick at my borrowing money from her. She thought it was all I was after.'

'You borrowed money from her!' said Francesca; 'you were fool enough to borrow money from a girl who was favourably disposed towards you, and with Courtenay Youghal in the background waiting to step in and oust you!'

Francesca's voice trembled with misery and rage. This great stroke of good luck that had seemed about to fall into their laps had been thrust aside by an act or series of acts of wanton paltry folly. The good ship had been lost for the sake of the traditional ha'p'orth of tar. Comus had paid some pressing tailor's or tobacconist's bill with a loan unwillingly put at his disposal by the girl he was courting, and had flung away his chances of securing a wealthy and in every way desirable bride. Elaine de Frey and her fortune might have been the making of Comus, but he had hurried in as usual to effect his own undoing. Calmness did not in this case come with reflection; the more Francesca thought about the matter, the more exasperated she grew. Comus threw himself down in a low chair and watched her without a trace of embarrassment or concern at her mortification. He had come to her feeling rather sorry for himself, and bitterly conscious of his defeat, and she had met him with a taunt and without the least hint of sympathy; he determined that she should be tantalized with the knowledge of how small and stupid a thing had stood between the realization and ruin of her hopes for him.

'And to think she should be captured by Courtenay Youghal,' said Francesca bitterly; 'I've always deplored your intimacy with that young man.'

'It's hardly my intimacy with him that's made Elaine accept him,' said Comus.

Francesca realized the futility of further upbraiding. Through the tears of vexation that stood in her eyes she looked across at the handsome boy who sat opposite her, mocking at his own misfortune, perversely indifferent to his folly, seemingly almost indifferent to its consequences.

'Comus,' she said quietly and wearily, 'you are an exact reversal of the legend of Pandora's Box. You have all the charm and advantages that a boy could want to help him on in the world, and behind it all there is the fatal damning gift of utter hopelessness.'

'I think,' said Comus, 'that is the best description that anyone has ever given of me.'

For the moment there was a flush of sympathy and something like outspoken affection between mother and son. They seemed very much alone in the world just now, and in the general overturn of hopes and plans there flickered a chance that each might stretch out a hand to the other, and summon back to their lives an old dead love that was the best and strongest feeling either of them had known. But the sting of disappointment was too keen, and the flood of resentment mounted too high on either side to allow the chance more than a moment in which to flicker away into nothingness. The old fatal topic of estrangement came to the fore, the question of immediate ways and means, and mother and son faced themselves again as antagonists on a well-disputed field.

'What is done is done,' said Francesca, with a movement of tragic impatience that belied the philosophy of her words; 'there is nothing to be gained by crying over spilt milk. There is the present and the future to be thought about, though. One can't go on indefinitely as a tenant-for-life in a fools' paradise.' Then she pulled herself together and proceeded to deliver an ultimatum which the force of circumstances no longer permitted her to hold in reserve.

'It's not much use talking to you about money, as I know from long experience, but I can only tell you this, that in the middle of the season I'm already obliged to be thinking of leaving town. And you, I'm afraid, will have to be thinking of leaving England at equally short notice. Henry told me the other day that he can get you something out in West Africa. You've had your chance of doing something better for yourself from the financial point of view, and you've thrown it away for the sake of borrowing a little ready money for your luxuries, so now you must take what you can get. The pay won't be very good at first, but living is not dear out there.'

'West Africa,' said Comus reflectively; 'it's a sort of modern substitute for the old-fashioned *oubliette*, a convenient depository for tiresome people. Dear Uncle Henry may talk lugubriously about the burden of Empire, but he evidently recognizes its uses as a refuse consumer.'

'My dear Comus, you are talking of the West Africa of yesterday. While you have been wasting your time at school, and worse than wasting your time in the West End, other people have been grappling with the study of tropical diseases, and the West African coast country is being rapidly transformed from a lethal chamber into a sanatorium.'

Comus laughed mockingly.

'What a beautiful bit of persuasive prose! It reminds one of the Psalms, and even more of a company prospectus. If you were honest you'd confess that you lifted it straight out of a rubber or railway promotion scheme. Seriously, mother, if I must grub about for a living, why can't I do it in England? I could go into a brewery, for instance.'

Francesca shook her head decisively; she could foresee the sort of steady work Comus was likely to accomplish, with the lodestone of town and the minor attractions of race-meetings and similar festivities always beckoning to him from a conveniently attainable distance, but apart from that aspect of the case there was a financial obstacle in the way of his obtaining any employment at home.

'Breweries and all those sort of things necessitate money to start with; one has to pay premiums or invest capital in the undertaking and so forth. And as we have no money available, and can scarcely pay our debts as it is, it's no use thinking about it.'

'Can't we sell something?' asked Comus.

He made no actual suggestion as to what should be sacrificed, but he was looking straight at the Van der Meulen.

For a moment Francesca felt a stifling sensation of weakness, as though her heart was going to stop beating. Then she sat forward in her chair and spoke with energy, almost fierceness.

'When I am dead my things can be sold and dispersed. As long as I am alive I prefer to keep them by me.'

In her holy place, with all her treasured possessions around her, this dreadful suggestion had been made. Some of her cherished household gods, souvenirs and keepsakes from past days, would, perhaps, not have fetched a very considerable sum in the auction-room, others had a distinct value of their own, but to her they were all precious. And the Van der Meulen, at which Comus had looked with impious appraising eyes, was the most sacred of them all. When Francesca had been away from her town residence or had been confined to her bedroom through illness, the great picture with its stately solemn representation of a long-ago battle-scene, painted to flatter the flattery-loving soul of a warrior-king who was dignified even in his campaigns—this was the first thing she visited on her return to town or convalescence. If an alarm of fire had been raised it would have been the first thing for whose safety she would have troubled. And Comus had almost suggested that it should be parted with, as one sold railway shares and other soulless things.

Scolding, she had long ago realized, was a useless waste of time and energy where Comus was concerned, but this evening she unloosed her tongue for the mere relief that it gave to her surcharged feelings. He sat listening without comment, though she purposely let fall remarks that she hoped might sting him into self-defence or protest. It was an unsparing indictment, the more damaging in that it was so irrefutably true, the more tragic in that it came from perhaps the one person in the world whose opinion he had ever cared for. And he sat through it as silent and seemingly unmoved as though she had been rehearsing a speech for some drawing-room comedy. When she had had her say his method of retort was not the soft answer that turneth away wrath, but the inconsequent one that shelves it.

'Let's go and dress for dinner.'

The meal, like so many that Francesca and Comus had eaten in each other's company of late, was a silent one. Now that the full bearings of the disaster had been discussed in all its aspects, there was nothing more to be said. Any attempt at ignoring the situation and passing on to less controversial topics would have been a mockery and pretence which neither of them would have troubled to sustain. So the meal went forward with its dragged-out dreary intimacy of two people who were separated by a gulf of bitterness, and whose hearts were hard with resentment against one another.

Francesca felt a sense of relief when she was able to give the maid the order to serve her coffee upstairs. Comus had a sullen scowl on his face, but he looked up as she rose to leave the room, and gave his half-mocking little laugh.

'You needn't look so tragic,' he said. 'You're going to have your own way. I'll go out to that West African hole.'

CHAPTER XIII

COMUS found his way to his seat in the stalls of the Straw Exchange Theatre, and turned to watch the stream of distinguished and distinguishable people who made their appearance as a matter of course at a First Night in the height of the season. Pit and gallery were already packed with a throng, tense, expectant and alert, that waited for the rise of the curtain with the eager patience of a terrier watching a dilatory human prepare for outdoor exercises. Stalls and boxes filled slowly and hesitatingly with a crowd whose component units seemed for the most part to recognize the probability that they were quite as interesting as any play they were likely to see. Those who bore no particular face-value themselves derived a certain amount of social dignity from the near neighbourhood of obvious notabilities; if one could not obtain recognition oneself there was some vague pleasure in being able to recognize notoriety at intimately close quarters.

'Who is that woman with the auburn hair and a rather effective belligerent gleam in her eyes?' asked a man sitting just behind Comus. 'She looks as if she might have created the world in six days and destroyed it on the seventh.'

'I forget her name,' said his neighbour; 'she writes. She's the author of that book, *The Woman Who Wished it was Wednesday*, you know. It used to be the convention that women writers should be plain and dowdy; now we have gone to the other extreme and build them on extravagantly decorative lines.'

A buzz of recognition came from the front rows of the pit, together with the craning of necks on the part of those in less favoured seats. It heralded the arrival of Sherard Blaw, the dramatist who had discovered himself, and who had given so ungrudgingly of his discovery to the world. Lady Caroline, who was already directing little conversational onslaughts from her box, gazed gently for a moment at the new arrival, and then turned to the silver-haired Archdeacon sitting beside her.

'They say the poor man is haunted by the fear that he will die during a general election, and that his obituary notices will be seriously curtailed by the space taken up by the election results. The curse of our party system, from his point of view, is that it takes up so much room in the Press.'

The Archdeacon smiled indulgently. As a man he was so exquisitely worldly that he fully merited the name of the Heavenly Worldling bestowed on him by an admiring duchess, and withal his texture was shot with a pattern of such genuine saintliness that one felt that whoever else might hold the keys of Paradise he, at least, possessed a private latchkey to that abode.

'Is it not significant of the altered grouping of things,' he observed, 'that the Church, as represented by me, sympathizes with the message of Sherard Blaw, while neither the man nor his message find acceptance with unbelievers like you, Lady Caroline?'

Lady Caroline blinked her eyes. 'My dear Archdeacon,' she said, 'no one can be an unbeliever nowadays. The Christian Apologists have left one nothing to disbelieve.'

The Archdeacon rose with a delighted chuckle. 'I must go and tell that to De la Poulett,' he said, indicating a clerical figure sitting in the third row of the stalls; 'he spends his life explaining from his pulpit that the glory of Christianity consists in the fact that though it is not true it has been found necessary to invent it.'

The door of the box opened and Courtenay Youghal entered, bringing with him a subtle suggestion of chaminade and an atmosphere of political tension. The Government had fallen out of the good graces of a section of its supporters, and those who were not in the know were busy predicting a serious crisis over a forthcoming division in the Committee stage of an important Bill. This was Saturday night, and unless some successful cajolery were effected between now and Monday afternoon, Ministers would be, seemingly, in danger of defeat.

'Ah, here is Youghal,' said the Archdeacon; 'he will be able to tell us what is going to happen in the next forty-eight hours. I hear the Prime Minister says it is a matter of conscience, and they will stand or fall by it.'

His hopes and sympathies were notoriously on the Ministerial side.

Youghal greeted Lady Caroline and subsided gracefully into a chair well in the front of the box. A buzz of recognition rippled slowly across the house.

'For the Government to fall on a matter of conscience' he said, 'would be like a man cutting himself with a safety razor.'

Lady Caroline purred a gentle approval.

'I'm afraid it's true, Archdeacon,' she said.

No one can effectively defend a Government when it's been in office several years. The Archdeacon took refuge in light skirmishing.

'I believe Lady Caroline sees the makings of a great Socialist statesman in you, Youghal,' he observed.

'Great Socialist statesmen aren't made, they're stillborn,' replied Youghal.

'What is the play about to-night?' asked a pale young woman who had taken no part in the talk.

'I don't know,' said Lady Caroline, 'but I hope it's dull. If there is any brilliant conversation in it I shall burst into tears.'

In the front row of the upper circle a woman with a restless starling-voice was discussing the work of a temporarily fashionable composer, chiefly in relation to her own emotions, which she seemed to think might prove generally interesting to those around her.

'Whenever I hear his music I feel that I want to go up into a mountain and pray. Can you understand that feeling?'

The girl to whom she was unburdening herself shook her head.

'You see, I've heard his music chiefly in Switzerland, and we were up among the mountains all the time, so it wouldn't have made any difference.'

'In that case,' said the woman, who seemed to have emergency emotions to suit all geographical conditions, 'I should have wanted to be in a great silent plain by the side of a rushing river.'

'What I think is so splendid about his music——' commenced another starling-voice on the farther side of the girl. Like sheep that feed greedily before the coming of a storm, the starling-voices seemed impelled to extra effort by the knowledge of four imminent intervals of acting during which they would be hushed into constrained silence.

In the back row of the dress circle a late-comer, after a cursory glance at the programme, had settled down into a comfortable narrative, which was evidently the resumed thread of an unfinished taxi-drive monologue.

'We all said, "It can't be Captain Parminter, because he's always been sweet on Joan," and then Emily said——'

The curtain went up, and Emily's contribution to the discussion had to held over till the entr'acte.

The play promised to be a success. The author, avoiding the pitfall of brilliancy, had aimed at being interesting; and as far as possible, bearing in mind that his play was a comedy, he had striven to be amusing. Above all he had remembered that in the laws of stage proportions it is permissible and generally desirable that the part should be greater than the whole; hence he had been careful to give the leading lady such a clear and commanding lead over the other characters of the play that it was impossible for any of them ever to get on level terms with her. The action of the piece was now and then delayed thereby, but the duration of its run would be materially prolonged.

The curtain came down on the first act amid an encouraging instalment of applause, and the audience turned its back on the stage and began to take a renewed interest in itself. The authoress of *The Woman Who Wished it was Wednesday* had swept like a convalescent whirlwind, subdued but potentially tempestuous, into Lady Caroline's box.

'I've just trodden with all my weight on the foot of an eminent publisher as I was leaving my seat,' she cried, with a peal of delighted laughter. 'He was such a dear about it; I said I hoped I hadn't hurt him, and he said, "I suppose you think, who drives hard bargains should himself be hard." Wasn't it pet lamb of him?'

'I've never trodden on a pet lamb,' said Lady Caroline, 'so I've no idea what its behaviour would be under the circumstances.'

'Tell me,' said the authoress, coming to the front of the box, the better to survey the house, and perhaps also with a charitable desire to make things easy for those who might pardonably wish to survey her, 'tell me, please, where is the girl sitting whom Courtenay Youghal is engaged to?'

Elaine was pointed out to her, sitting in the fourth row of the stalls, on the opposite side of the house to where Comus had his seat. Once during the interval she had turned to give him a friendly nod of recognition as he stood in one of the side gangways, but he was absorbed at the moment in looking at himself in the glass panel. The grave brown eyes and the mocking green-grey ones had looked their last into each other's depths.

For Comus this first-night performance, with its brilliant gathering of spectators, its groups and coteries of lively talkers, even its counterfoil of dull chatterers, its pervading atmosphere of stage and social movement, and its intruding undercurrent of political flutter, all this composed a tragedy in which he was the chief character. It was the life he knew and loved and basked in, and it was the life he was leaving. It would go on reproducing itself again and again, with its stage interest and social interest and intruding outside interests, with the same lively chattering crowd, the people who had done things being pointed out by people who recognized them to people who didn't—it would all go on with unflagging animation and sparkle and enjoyment, and for him it would have stopped utterly. He would be in some unheard-of sun-blistered wilderness, where natives and pariah dogs and raucous-throated crows fringed round mockingly on one's loneliness, where one rode for sweltering miles for the chance of meeting a collector or police officer, with whom most likely on closer acquaintance one had hardly two ideas in common, where female society was represented at long intervals by some climate-withered woman missionary or official's wife, where food and sickness and veterinary lore became at last the three outstanding subjects on which the mind settled, or rather sank. That was the life he foresaw and dreaded, and that was the life he was going to. For a boy who went out to it from the dullness of some country rectory, from a neighbourhood where a flower show and a cricket match formed the social landmarks of the year, the feeling of exile might not be very crushing, might indeed be lost in the sense of change and adventure. But Comus had lived too thoroughly in the centre of things to regard life in a backwater as anything else than stagnation, and stagnation while one is young he justly regarded as an offence against nature and reason, in keeping with the perverted mockery that sends decrepit invalids touring painfully about the world and shuts panthers up in narrow cages. He was being put aside, as a wine is put aside, but to deteriorate instead of gaining in the process, to lose the best time of his youth and health and good looks in a world where youth and health and good looks count for much and where time never returns lost possessions. And thus, as the curtain swept down on the close of each act, Comus felt a sense of depression and deprivation sweep down on himself; bitterly he watched his last evening of social gaiety slipping away to its end. In less than an hour it would be over; in a few months' time it would be an unreal memory.

In the third interval, as he gazed round at the chattering house, someone touched him on the arm. It was Lady Veula Croot.

'I suppose in a week's time you'll be on the high seas?' she said. 'I'm coming to your farewell dinner, you know; your mother has just asked me. I'm not going to talk the usual rot to you about how much you will like it and so on. I sometimes think that one of the advantages of hell will be that no one will have the impertinence to point out to you that you're really better off than you would be anywhere else. What do you think of the play? Of course one can foresee the end; she will come to her husband with the announcement that their longed-for child is going to be born, and that will smooth over everything. So conveniently effective to wind up a comedy with the commencement of someone else's tragedy. And everyone will go away saying, "I'm glad it had a happy ending." '

Lady Veula moved back to her seat, with her pleasant smile on her lips and the look of infinite weariness in her eyes.

The interval, the last interval, was drawing to a close, and the house began to turn with fidgety attention towards the stage for the unfolding of the final phase of the play. Francesca sat in Serena Golackly's box listening to Colonel Springfield's story of what happened to a pigeon-cote in his compound at Poona. Everyone who knew the Colonel had to listen to that story a good many times, but Lady Caroline had mitigated the boredom of the infliction, and in fact invested it with a certain sporting interest, by offering a prize to the person who heard it oftenest in the course of the season, the competitors being under an honourable understanding not to lead up to the subject. Ada Spelvexit and a boy in the Foreign Office were at present at the top of the list with five recitals each to their score, but the former was suspected of doubtful adherence to the rules and spirit of the competition.

'And there, dear lady,' concluded the Colonel, 'were the eleven dead pigeons. What had become of the bandicoot no one ever knew.'

Francesca thanked him for his story, and complacently inscribed the figure 4 on the margin of her theatre programme. Almost at the same moment she heard George St Michael's voice pattering out a breathless piece of intelligence for the edification of Serena Golackly and anyone else who might care to listen. Francesca galvanized into sudden attention.

'Emmeline Chetrof to a fellow in the Indian Forest Department. He's got nothing but his pay, and they can't be married for four or five years: an absurdly long engagement, don't you think so? All very well to wait seven years for a wife in patriarchal times when you probably had others to go on with, and you lived long enough to celebrate your own tercentenary, but under modern conditions it seems a foolish arrangement.'

St Michael spoke almost with a sense of grievance. A marriage project that tied up all the small pleasant nuptial gossip-items about bridesmaids and honeymoon and recalcitrant aunts and so forth for an indefinite number of years seemed scarcely decent in his eyes, and there was little satisfaction or importance to be derived from early and special knowledge of an event which loomed as far distant as a Presidential Election or a change of Viceroy. But to Francesca, who had listened with startled apprehension at the mention of Emmeline Chetrof's name, the news came in a flood of relief and thankfulness. Short of entering a nunnery and taking celibate vows, Emmeline could hardly have behaved more conveniently than in tying herself up to a lover whose circumstances made it necessary to relegate marriage to the distant future. For four or five years Francesca was assured of undisturbed possession of the house in Blue Street, and after that period who knew what might happen? The engagement might stretch on indefinitely, it might even come to nothing under the weight of its accumulated years, as sometimes happened with these protracted affairs. Emmeline might lose her fancy for her absentee lover, and might never replace him with another. A golden possibility of perpetual tenancy of her present home began to float once more through Francesca's mind. As long as Emmeline had been unbespoken in the marriage market there had always been the haunting likelihood of seeing the dreaded announcement, 'A marriage has been arranged and will shortly take place', in connection with her name. And now a marriage had been arranged and would *not* shortly take place, might indeed never take place. St Michael's information was likely to be correct in this instance; he would never have invented a piece of matrimonial intelligence which gave such little scope for supplementary detail of the kind he loved to supply. As Francesca turned to watch the fourth act of the play, her mind was singing a pæan of thankfulness and exultation. It was as though some artificer sent by the gods had reinforced with a substantial cord the horsehair thread that held up the sword of Damocles over her head. Her love for her home, for her treasured household possessions and her pleasant social life, was able to expand once more in present security, and feed on future hope. She was still young enough to count four or five years as a long time, and to-night she was optimistic enough to prophesy smooth things of the future that lay beyond that span. Of the fourth act, with its carefully held back but obviously imminent reconciliation between the leading characters, she took in but little, except that she vaguely understood it to have a happy ending. As the lights went up she looked round on the dispersing audience with a feeling of friendliness uppermost in her mind; even the sight of Elaine de Frey and Courtenay Youghal leaving the theatre together did not inspire her with a tenth part of the annoyance that their entrance had caused her. Serena's invitation to go on to the Savoy for supper fitted in exactly with her mood of exhilaration. It would be a fit and appropriate wind-up to an auspicious evening. The cold chicken and modest brand of Chablis waiting for her at home should give way to a banquet of more festive nature.

In the crush of the vestibule, friends and enemies, personal and political, were jostled and locked together in the general effort to rejoin temporarily estranged garments and secure the attendance of elusive vehicles. Lady Caroline found herself at close quarters with the estimable Henry Greech, and experienced some of the joy which comes to the homeward-wending sportsman when a chance shot presents itself on which he may expend his remaining cartridges.

'So the Government is going to climb down, after all,' she said, with a provocative assumption of private information on the subject.

'I assure you the Government will do nothing of the kind,' replied the Member of Parliament with befitting dignity; 'the Prime Minister told me last night that under no circumstances——'

'My dear Mr Greech,' said Lady Caroline, 'we all know that Prime Ministers are wedded to the truth, but like other wedded couples they sometimes live apart.'

For her, at any rate, the comedy had had a happy ending.

Comus made his way slowly and lingeringly from the stalls, so slowly that the lights were already being turned down and great shroud-like dust-cloths were being swathed over the ornamental gilt-work. The laughing, chattering, yawning throng had filtered out of the vestibule, and was melting away in final groups from the steps of the theatre. An impatient attendant gave him his coat and locked up the cloak-room. Comus stepped out under the portico; he looked at the posters announcing the play, and in anticipation he could see other posters announcing its 200th performance. Two hundred performances; by that time the Straw Exchange Theatre would be to him something so remote and unreal that it would hardly seem to exist or to have ever existed except in his fancy. And to the laughing, chattering throng that would pass in under that portico to the 200th performance, he would be, to those that had known him, something equally remote and non-existent. 'The good-looking Bassington boy? Oh, dead, or rubber-growing or sheep-farming, or something of that sort.'

CHAPTER XIV

THE farewell dinner which Francesca had hurriedly organized in honour of her son's departure threatened from the outset to be a doubtfully successful function. In the first place, as he observed privately, there was very little of Comus and a good deal of farewell in it. His own particular friends were unrepresented. Courtenay Youghal was out of the question; and though Francesca would have stretched a point and welcomed some of his other male associates of whom she scarcely approved, he himself had been opposed to including any of them in the invitations. On the other hand, as Henry Greech had provided Comus with this job that he was going out to, and was, moreover, finding part of the money for the necessary outfit, Francesca had felt it her duty to ask him and his wife to the dinner; the obtuseness that seems to cling to some people like a garment throughout their life had caused Mr Greech to accept the invitation. When Comus heard of the circumstances he laughed long and boisterously; his spirits, Francesca noted, seemed to be rising fast as the hour for departure drew near.

The other guests included Serena Golackly and Lady Veula, the latter having been asked on the inspiration of the moment at the theatrical first night. In the height of the season it was not easy to get together a goodly selection of guests at short notice, and Francesca had gladly fallen in with Serena's suggestion of bringing with her Stephen Thorle, who was alleged, in loose feminine phrasing, to 'know all about' tropical Africa. His travels and experiences in those regions probably did not cover much ground or stretch over any great length of time, but he was one of those individuals who can describe a continent on the strength of a few days' stay in a coast town as intimately and dogmatically as a palæontologist will reconstruct an extinct mammal from the evidence of a stray shin-bone. He had the loud penetrating voice and the prominent penetrating eyes of a man who can do no listening in the ordinary way and whose eyes have to perform the function of listening for him. His vanity did not necessarily make him unbearable, unless one had to spend much time in his society, and his need for a wide field of audience and admiration was mercifully calculated to spread his operations over a considerable human area. Moreover, his craving for attentive listeners forced him to interest himself in a wonderful variety of subjects on which he was able to discourse fluently and with a certain semblance of special knowledge. Politics he avoided; the ground was too well known, and there was a definite No to every definite Yes that could be put forward. Moreover, argument was not congenial to his disposition, which preferred an unchallenged flow of dissertation modified by occasional helpful questions which formed the starting-point for new offshoots of word-spinning. The promotion of cottage industries, the prevention of juvenile street trading, the extension of the Borstal prison system, the furtherance of vague talkative religious movements, the fostering of inter-racial *ententes*, all found in him a tireless exponent, a fluent and entertaining, though perhaps not very convincing, advocate. With the real motive power behind these various causes he was not very closely identified; to the spade-workers who carried on the actual labours of each particular movement he bore the relation of a trowel-worker, delving superficially at the surface, but able to devote a proportionately far greater amount of time to the advertisement of his progress and achievements. Such was Stephen Thorle, a governess in the nursery of Chelsea-bred religions, a skilled window-dresser in the emporium of his own personality, and needless to say, evanescently popular amid a wide but shifting circle of acquaintances. He improved on the record of a socially much-travelled individual whose experience has become classical, and went to most of the best houses—twice.

His inclusion as a guest at this particular dinner-party was not a very happy inspiration. He was inclined to patronize Comus, as well as the African continent, and on even slighter acquaintance. With the exception of Henry Greech, whose feelings towards his nephew had been soured by many years of overt antagonism, there was an uncomfortable feeling among those present that the topic of the black-sheep export trade, as Comus would have himself expressed it, was being given undue prominence in what should have been a festive farewell banquet. And Comus, in whose honour the feast was given, did not contribute much towards its success; though his spirits seemed strung up to a high pitch, his merriment was more the merriment of a cynical and amused onlooker than of one who responds to the gaiety of his companions. Sometimes he laughed quietly to himself at some chance remark of a scarcely mirth-provoking nature, and Lady Veula, watching him narrowly, came to the conclusion that an element of fear was blended with his seemingly buoyant spirits. Once or twice he caught her eye across the table, and a certain sympathy seemed to grow up between them, as though they were both consciously watching some lugubrious comedy that was being played out before them.

An untoward little incident had marked the commencement of the meal. A small still-life picture that hung over the sideboard had snapped its cord and slid down with an alarming clatter on to the crowded board beneath it. The picture itself was scarcely damaged, but its fall had been accompanied by a tinkle of broken glass, and it was found that a liqueur glass, one out of a set of seven that would be impossible to match, had been shivered into fragments. Francesca's almost motherly love for her possessions made her peculiarly sensible to a feeling of annoyance and depression at the accident, but she turned politely to listen to Mrs Greech's account of a misfortune in which four soup-plates were involved. Mrs Henry was not a brilliant conversationalist, and her flank was speedily turned by Stephen Thorle, who recounted a slum experience in which two entire families did all their feeding out of one damaged soup-plate.

'The gratitude of those poor creatures when I presented them with a set of table crockery apiece, the tears in their eyes and in their voices when they thanked me, would be impossible to describe.'

'Thank you all the same for describing it,' said Comus.

The listening eyes went swiftly round the table to gather evidence as to how this rather disconcerting remark had been received, but Thorle's voice continued uninterruptedly to retail stories of East End gratitude, never failing to mention the particular deeds of disinterested charity on his part which had evoked and

justified the gratitude. Mrs Greech had to suppress the interesting sequel to her broken crockery narrative, to wit, how she subsequently matched the shattered soup-plates at Harrod's. Like an imported plant species that sometimes flourishes exceedingly, and makes itself at home to the dwarfing and overshadowing of all native species, Thorle dominated the dinner-party and thrust its original purport somewhat into the background. Serena began to look helplessly apologetic. It was altogether rather a relief when the filling of champagne glasses gave Francesca an excuse for bringing matters back to their intended footing.

'We must all drink a health,' she said. 'Comus, my own dear boy, a safe and happy voyage to you, much prosperity in the life you are going out to, and in due time a safe and happy return——'

Her hand gave an involuntary jerk in the act of raising the glass, and the wine went streaming across the tablecloth in a froth of yellow bubbles. It certainly was not turning out a comfortable or auspicious dinner-party.

'My dear mother,' cried Comus, 'you must have been drinking healths all the afternoon to make your hand so unsteady.'

He laughed gaily and with apparent carelessness, but again Lady Veula caught the frightened note in his laughter. Mrs Henry, with practical sympathy, was telling Francesca two good ways for getting wine-stains out of tablecloths. The smaller economies of life were an unnecessary branch of learning for Mrs Greech, but she studied them as carefully and conscientiously as a stay-at-home plain-dwelling English child commits to memory the measurements and altitudes of the world's principal peaks. Some women of her temperament and mentality know by heart the favourite colours, flowers, and hymn-tunes of all the members of the Royal Family; Mrs Greech would possibly have failed in an examination of that nature, but she knew what to do with carrots that have been over-long in storage.

Francesca did not renew her speech-making; a chill seemed to have fallen over all efforts at festivity, and she contented herself with refilling her glass and simply drinking to her boy's good health. The others followed her example, and Comus drained his glass with a brief 'Thank you all very much.' The sense of constraint which hung over the company was not, however, marked by any uncomfortable pause in the conversation. Henry Greech was a fluent thinker, of the kind that prefer to do their thinking aloud; the silence that descended on him as a mantle in the House of Commons was an official livery of which he divested himself as thoroughly as possible in private life. He did not propose to sit through dinner as a mere listener to Mr Thorle's personal narrative of philanthropic movements and experiences, and took the first opportunity of launching himself into a flow of satirical observations on current political affairs. Lady Veula was inured to this sort of thing in her own home circle, and sat listening with the stoical indifference with which an Eskimo might accept the occurrence of one snowstorm the more, in the course of an Arctic winter. Serena Golackly felt a certain relief at the fact that her imported guest was not, after all, monopolizing the conversation. But the latter was too determined a personality to allow himself to be thrust aside for many minutes by the talkative M.P. Henry Greech paused for an instant to chuckle at one of his own shafts of satire, and immediately Thorle's penetrating voice swept across the table.

'Oh, you politicians!' he exclaimed, with pleasant superiority; 'you are always fighting about how things should be done, and the consequence is you are never able to do anything. Would you like me to tell you what a Unitarian horse-dealer said to me at Brindisi about politicians?'

A Unitarian horse-dealer at Brindisi had all the allurement of the unexpected. Henry Greech's witticisms at the expense of the Front Opposition bench were destined to remain as unfinished as his wife's history of the broken soup-plates. Thorle was primed with an ample succession of stories and themes, chiefly concerning poverty, thriftlessness, reclamation, reformed characters, and so forth, which carried him in an almost uninterrupted sequence through the remainder of the dinner.

'What I want to do is to make people think,' he said, turning his prominent eyes on to his hostess; 'it's so hard to make people think.'

'At any rate you give them the opportunity,' said Comus cryptically.

As the ladies rose to leave the table Comus crossed over to pick up one of Lady Veula's gloves that had fallen to the floor.

'I did not know you kept a dog,' said Lady Veula.

'We don't,' said Comus, 'there isn't one in the house.'

'I could have sworn I saw one follow you across the hall this evening,' she said.

'A small black dog, something like a schipperke?' asked Comus in a low voice.

'Yes, that was it.'

'I saw it myself to-night; it ran from behind my chair just as I was sitting down. Don't say anything to the others about it; it would frighten my mother.'

'Have you ever seen it before?' Lady Veula asked quickly.

'Once, when I was six years old. It followed my father downstairs.'

Lady Veula said nothing. She knew that Comus had lost his father at the age of six.

In the drawing-room Serena made nervous excuses for her talkative friend.

'Really, rather an interesting man, you know, and up to the eyes in all sorts of movements. Just the sort of person to turn loose at a drawing-room meeting, or to send down to a mission-hall in some unheard-of neighbourhood. Given a sounding-board and a harmonium, and a titled woman of some sort in the chair, and he'll be perfectly happy; I must say I hadn't realized how overpowering he might be at a small dinner-party.'

'I should say he was a very good man,' said Mrs Greech; she had forgiven the mutilation of her soup-plate story.

The party broke up early, as most of the guests had other engagements to keep. With a belated recognition of the farewell nature of the occasion they made pleasant little good-bye remarks to Comus, with the usual predictions of prosperity and anticipations of an ultimate auspicious return. Even Henry Greech sank his personal dislike of the boy for the moment, and made hearty jocular allusions to a home-coming, which, in the elder man's eyes, seemed possibly pleasantly remote. Lady Veula alone made no reference to the future; she simply said, 'Good-bye, Comus,' but her voice was the kindest of all, and he responded with a look of gratitude. The weariness in her eyes was more marked than ever as she lay back against the cushions of her carriage.

'What a tragedy life is!' she said aloud to herself.

Serena and Stephen Thorle were the last to leave, and Francesca stood alone for a moment at the head of the stairway watching Comus laughing and chatting as he escorted the departing guests to the door. The ice-wall was melting under the influence of coming separation, and never had he looked more adorably handsome in her eyes, never had his merry laugh and mischief-loving gaiety seemed more infectious than on this night of his farewell banquet. She was glad enough that he was going away from a life of idleness and extravagance and temptation, but she began to suspect that she would miss, for a little while at any rate, the high-spirited boy who could be so attractive in his better moods. Her impulse, after the guests had gone, was to call him to her and hold him once more in her arms, and repeat her wishes for his happiness and good-luck in the land he was going to, and her promise of his welcome back, some not too distant day, to the land he was leaving. She wanted to forget, and to make him forget, the months of irritable jangling and sharp discussions, the months of cold aloofness and indifference, and to remember only that he was her own dear Comus as in the days of yore, before he had grown from an unmanageable pickle into a weariful problem. But she feared lest she should break down, and she did not wish to cloud his light-hearted gaiety on the very eve of his departure. She watched him for a moment as he stood in the hall, settling his tie before a mirror, and then went quietly back to her drawing-room. It had not been a very successful dinner-party, and the general effect it had left on her was one of depression.

Comus, with a lively musical-comedy air on his lips, and a look of wretchedness in his eyes, went out to visit the haunts that he was leaving so soon.

CHAPTER XV

ELAINE YOUGHAL sat at lunch in the Speise Saal of one of Vienna's costlier hotels. The double-headed eagle, with its 'K.u.K.' legend, everywhere met the eye and announced the imperial favour in which the establishment basked. Some several square yards of yellow bunting, charged with the image of another double-headed eagle, floating from the highest flagstaff above the building, betrayed to the initiated the fact that a Russian Grand Duke was concealed somewhere on the premises. Unannounced by heraldic symbolism, but unconcealable by reason of nature's own blazonry, were several citizens and citizenesses of the great republic of the Western world. One or two Cobdenite members of the British Parliament, engaged in the useful task of proving that the cost of living in Vienna was on an exorbitant scale, flitted with restrained importance through a land whose fatness they had come to spy out; every fancied overcharge in their bills was welcome as providing another nail in the coffin of their fiscal opponents. It is the glory of democracies that they may be misled, but never driven. Here and there, like brave deeds in a dust-patterned world, flashed and glittered the sumptuous uniforms of representatives of the Austrian military caste. Also in evidence, at discreet intervals, were stray units of the Semitic tribe that nineteen centuries of European neglect had been unable to mislay.

Elaine, sitting with Courtenay at an elaborately appointed luncheon table, gay with high goblets of Bohemian glassware, was mistress of three discoveries. First, to her disappointment, that if you frequent the more expensive hotels of Europe you must be prepared to find, in whatever country you may chance to be staying, a depressing international likeness between them all. Secondly, to her relief, that one is not expected to be sentimentally amorous during a modern honeymoon. Thirdly, rather to her dismay, that Courtenay Youghal did not necessarily expect her to be markedly affectionate in private. Someone had described him, after their

127

marriage, as one of Nature's bachelors, and she began to see how aptly the description fitted him.

'Will those Germans on our left never stop talking?' she asked, as an undying flow of Teutonic small-talk rattled and jangled across the intervening stretch of carpet. 'Not one of those three women has ceased talking for an instant since we've been sitting here.'

'They will presently, if only for a moment,' said Courtenay; 'when the dish you have ordered comes in there will be a deathly silence at the next table. No German can see a *plat* brought in for someone else without being possessed with a great fear that it represents a more toothsome morsel or a better money's worth than what he has ordered for himself.'

The exuberant Teutonic chatter was balanced on the other side of the room by an even more penetrating conversation unflaggingly maintained by a party of Americans, who were sitting in judgment on the cuisine of the country they were passing through, and finding few extenuating circumstances.

'What Mr Lonkins wants is a real *deep* cherry pie,' announced a lady in a tone of dramatic and honest conviction.

'Why, yes, that is so,' corroborated a gentleman who was apparently the Mr Lonkins in question; 'a real *deep* cherry pie.'

'We had the same trouble way back in Paris,' proclaimed another lady; 'little Jerome and the girls don't want to eat any more *crème renversée*. I'd give anything if they could get some real cherry pie.'

'Real *deep* cherry pie,' assented Mr Lonkins.

'Way down in Ohio we used to have peach pie that was real good,' said Mrs Lonkins, turning on a tap of reminiscence that presently flowed to a cascade. The subject of pies seemed to lend itself to indefinite expansion.

'Do those people think of nothing but their food?' asked Elaine, as the virtues of roasted mutton suddenly came to the fore and received emphatic recognition, even the absent and youthful Jerome being quoted in its favour.

'On the contrary,' said Courtenay, 'they are a widely-travelled set, and the man has had a notably interesting career. It is a form of homesickness with them to discuss and lament the cookery and foods that they've never had the leisure to stay at home and digest. The Wandering Jew probably babbled unremittingly about some breakfast dish that took so long to prepare that he had never time to eat it.'

A waiter deposited a dish of Wiener Nierenbraten in front of Elaine. At the same moment a magic hush fell upon the three German ladies at the adjoining table, and the flicker of a great fear passed across their eyes. Then they burst forth again into tumultuous chatter. Courtenay had proved a reliable prophet.

Almost at the same moment as the luncheon-dish appeared on the scene, two ladies arrived at a neighbouring table, and bowed with dignified cordiality to Elaine and Courtenay. They were two of the more worldly and travelled of Elaine's extensive stock of aunts, and they happened to be making a short stay at the same hotel as the young couple. They were far too correct and rationally minded to intrude themselves on their niece, but it was significant of Elaine's altered view as to the sanctity of honeymoon life that she secretly rather welcomed the presence of her two relatives in the hotel, and had found time and occasion to give them more of her society than she would have considered necessary or desirable a few weeks ago. The younger of the two she rather liked, in a restrained fashion, as one likes an unpretentious watering-place or a restaurant that does not try to give one a musical education in addition to one's dinner. One felt instinctively about her that she would never wear rather more valuable diamonds than any other woman in the room, and would never be the only person to be saved in a steamboat disaster or hotel fire. As a child she might have been perfectly well able to recite 'On Linden when the sun was low', but one felt certain that nothing ever induced her to do so. The elder aunt, Mrs Goldbrook, did not share her sister's character as a human rest-cure; most people found her rather disturbing, chiefly, perhaps, from her habit of asking unimportant questions with enormous solemnity. Her manner of inquiring after a trifling ailment gave one the impression that she was more concerned with the fortunes of the malady than with oneself, and when one got rid of a cold one felt that she almost expected to be given its postal address. Probably her manner was merely the defensive outwork of an innate shyness, but she was not a woman who commanded confidences.

'A telephone call for Courtenay,' commented the younger of the two women as Youghal hurriedly flashed through the room; 'the telephone system seems to enter very largely into the young man's life.'

'The telephone has robbed matrimony of most of its sting,' said the elder; 'so much more discreet than pen and ink communications which get read by the wrong people.'

Elaine's aunts were conscientiously worldly; they were the natural outcome of a stock that had been conscientiously strait-laced for many generations.

Elaine had progressed to the pancake stage before Courtenay returned.

'Sorry to be away so long,' he said, 'but I've arranged something rather nice for to-night. There's rather a jolly masquerade ball on. I've 'phoned about getting a costume for you, and it's all right. It will suit you beautifully, and I've got my harlequin dress with me. Madame Kelnicort, excellent soul, is going to chaperone you, and she'll take you back any time you like; I'm quite unreliable when I get into fancy dress. I shall probably keep going till some unearthly hour of the morning.'

A masquerade ball in a strange city hardly represented Elaine's idea of enjoyment. Carefully to disguise one's identity in a neighbourhood where one was entirely unknown seemed to her rather meaningless. With Courtenay, of course, it was different; he seemed to have friends and acquaintances everywhere. However, the matter had progressed to a point which would have made a refusal to go seem rather ungracious. Elaine finished her pancake and began to take a polite interest in her costume.

'What is your character?' asked Madame Kelnicort that evening, as they uncloaked, preparatory to entering the already crowded ballroom.

'I believe I'm supposed to represent Marjolaine de Montfort, whoever she may have been,' said Elaine. 'Courtenay declares he only wanted to marry me because I'm his ideal of her.'

'But what a mistake to go as a character you know nothing about. To enjoy a masquerade ball you ought to throw away your own self and be the character you represent. Now Courtenay has been Harlequin since half-way through dinner; I could see it dancing in his eyes. At about six o'clock to-morrow morning he will fall asleep and wake up a member of the British House of Parliament on his honeymoon, but to-night he is unrestrainedly Harlequin.'

Elaine stood in the ball-room surrounded by a laughing, jostling throng of pierrots, jockeys, Dresden-china shepherdesses, Rumanian peasant-girls, and all the lively make-believe creatures that form the ingredients of a fancy-dress ball. As she stood watching them she experienced a growing feeling of annoyance, chiefly with herself. She was assisting, as the French say, at one of the gayest scenes of Europe's gayest capital, and she was conscious of being absolutely unaffected by the gaiety around her. The costumes were certainly interesting to look at, and the music good to listen to, and to that extent she was amused, but the *abandon* of the scene made no appeal to her. It was like watching a game of which you did not know the rules, and in the issue of which you were not interested. Elaine began to wonder what was the earliest moment at which she could drag Madame Kelnicort away from the revel without being guilty of sheer cruelty. Then Courtenay wriggled out of the crush and came towards her, a joyous, laughing Courtenay, looking younger and handsomer than she had ever seen him. She could scarcely recognize in him to-night the rising young debater who made embarrassing onslaughts on the Government's foreign policy before a crowded House of Commons. He claimed her for the dance that was just starting, and steered her dexterously into the heart of the waltzing crowd.

'You look more like Marjolaine than I should have thought a mortal woman of these days could look,' he declared, 'only Marjolaine did smile sometimes. You have rather the air of wondering if you'd left out enough tea for the servants' breakfast. Don't mind my teasing; I love you to look like that, and besides, it makes a splendid foil to my Harlequin—my selfishness coming to the fore again, you see. But you really are to go home the moment you're bored; the excellent Kelnicort gets heaps of dances throughout the winter, so don't mind sacrificing her.'

A little later in the evening Elaine found herself standing out a dance with a grave young gentleman from the Russian Embassy.

'Monsieur Courtenay enjoys himself, doesn't he?' he observed, as the youthful-looking harlequin flashed past them, looking like some restless gorgeous-hued dragon-fly. 'Why is it that the good God has given your countrymen the boon of eternal youth? Some of your countrywomen, too, but all of the men.'

Elaine could think of many of her countrymen who were not and never could have been youthful, but as far as Courtenay was concerned she recognized the fitness of the remark. And the recognition carried with it a sense of depression. Would he always remain youthful and keen on gaiety and revelling, while she grew staid and retiring? She had thrust the lively intractable Comus out of her mind, as by his perverseness he had thrust himself out of her heart, and she had chosen the brilliant young man of affairs as her husband. He had honestly let her see the selfish side of his character while he was courting her, but she had been prepared to make due sacrifices to the selfishness of a public man who had his career to consider above all other things. Would she also have to make sacrifices to the harlequin spirit which was now revealing itself as an undercurrent in his nature? When one has inured oneself to the idea of a particular form of victimization it is disconcerting to be confronted with another. Many a man who would patiently undergo martyrdom for religion's sake would be furiously unwilling to be a martyr to neuralgia.

'I think that is why you English love animals so much,' pursued the young diplomat; 'you are such splendid animals yourselves. You are lively because you want to be lively, not because people are looking on at you. Monsieur Courtenay is certainly an animal. I mean it as a high compliment.'

'Am I an animal?' asked Elaine.

'I was going to say you are an angel,' said the Russian, in some embarrassment, 'but I do not think that would do; angels and animals would never get on together. To get on with animals you must have a sense of humour, and I don't suppose angels have any sense of humour; you see it would be no use to them as they never hear any jokes.'

'Perhaps,' said Elaine, with a tinge of bitterness in her voice, 'perhaps I am a vegetable.'

'I think you most remind me of a picture,' said the Russian.

It was not the first time Elaine had heard the simile.

'I know,' she said, 'the Narrow Gallery at the Louvre: attributed to Leonardo da Vinci.'

Evidently the impression she made on people was solely one of externals.

Was that how Courtenay regarded her? Was that to be her function and place in life, a painted background, a decorative setting to other people's triumphs and tragedies? Somehow to-night she had the feeling that a general might have who brought imposing forces into the field and could do nothing with them. She possessed youth and good looks, considerable wealth, and had just made what would be thought by most people a very satisfactory marriage. And already she seemed to be standing aside as an onlooker where she had expected herself to be taking a leading part.

'Does this sort of thing appeal to you?' she asked the young Russian, nodding towards the gay scrimmage of masqueraders and rather prepared to hear an amused negative.

'But yes, of course,' he answered; 'costume balls, fancy fairs, café chantant, casino, anything that is not real life appeals to us Russians. Real life with us is the sort of thing that Maxim Gorki deals in. It interests us immensely, but we like to get away from it sometimes.'

Madame Kelnicort came up with another prospective partner, and Elaine delivered her ukase: one more dance and then back to the hotel. Without any special regret she made her retreat from the revel which Courtenay was enjoying under the impression that it was life and the young Russian under the firm conviction that it was not.

Elaine breakfasted at her aunts' table the next morning at much her usual hour. Courtenay was sleeping the sleep of a happy tired animal. He had given instructions to be called at eleven o'clock, from which time onward the *Neue Freie Presse*, the *Zeit*, and his toilet would occupy his attention till he appeared at the luncheon table. There were not many people breakfasting when Elaine arrived on the scene, but the room seemed to be fuller than it really was by reason of a penetrating voice that was engaged in recounting how far the standard of Viennese breakfast fare fell below the expectations and desires of little Jerome and the girls.

'If ever little Jerome becomes President of the United States,' said Elaine, 'I shall be able to contribute quite an informing article on his gastronomic likes and dislikes to the papers.'

The aunts were discreetly inquisitive as to the previous evening's entertainment.

'If Elaine would flirt mildly with somebody it would be such a good thing,' said Mrs Goldbrook; 'it would remind Courtenay that he's not the only attractive young man in the world.'

Elaine, however, did not gratify their hopes; she referred to the ball with the detachment she would have shown in describing a drawing-room show of cottage industries. It was not difficult to discern in her description of the affair the confession that she had been slightly bored. From Courtenay, later in the day, the aunts received a much livelier impression of the festivities, from which it was abundantly clear that he, at any rate, had managed to amuse himself. Neither did it appear that his good opinion of his own attractions had suffered any serious shock. He was distinctly in a very good temper.

'The secret of enjoying a honeymoon,' said Mrs Goldbrook afterwards to her sister, 'is not to attempt too much.'

'You mean——?'

'Courtenay is content to try and keep one person amused and happy, and he thoroughly succeeds.'

'I certainly don't think Elaine is going to be very happy,' said her sister, 'but at least Courtenay saved her from making the greatest mistake she could have made—marrying that young Bassington.'

'He has also,' said Mrs Goldbrook, 'helped her to make the next biggest mistake of her life—marrying Courtenay Youghal.'

CHAPTER XVI

IT was late afternoon by the banks of a swiftly rushing river, a river that gave back a haze of heat from its waters as though it were some stagnant steaming lagoon, and yet seemed to be whirling onward with the determination of a living thing, perpetually eager and remorseless, leaping savagely at any obstacle that attempted to stay its course; an unfriendly river, to whose waters you committed yourself at your peril. Under the hot breathless shade of the trees on its shore arose that acrid all-pervading smell that seems to hang everywhere about the tropics, a smell as of some monstrous musty still-room where herbs and spices have been crushed and distilled and stored for hundreds of years, and where the windows have seldom been opened. In the dazzling heat that still held undisputed sway over the scene, insects and birds seemed preposterously alive and active, flitting their gay colours through the sunbeams, and crawling over the baked dust in the full swing and pursuit of their several businesses; the flies engaged in Heaven knows what, and the fly-catchers busy with the flies. Beasts and humans showed no such indifference to the temperature; the sun would have to slant yet farther downward before the earth would become a fit arena for their revived activities. In the sheltered basement of a wayside rest-house a gang of native hammock-bearers slept or chattered drowsily through the last hours of the long midday halt; wide awake, yet almost motionless in the thrall of a heavy lassitude, their European master sat alone in an upper chamber, staring out through a narrow window-opening at the native village, spreading away in thick clusters of huts girt around with cultivated vegetation. It seemed a vast human ant-hill, which would presently be astir with its teeming human life, as though the Sun God in his last departing stride had roused it with a careless kick. Even as Comus watched he could see the beginnings of the evening's awakening. Women, squatting in front of their huts, began to pound away at the rice or maize that would form the evening meal, girls were collecting their water-pots preparatory to a walk down to the river, and enterprising goats made tentative forays through gaps in the ill-kept fences of neighbouring garden-plots; their hurried retreats showed that here at least someone was keeping alert and wakeful vigil. Behind a hut perched on a steep hill-side, just opposite to the rest-house, two boys were splitting wood with a certain languid industry; farther down the road a group of dogs were leisurely working themselves up to quarrelling pitch. Here and there, bands of evil-looking pigs roamed about, busy with foraging excursions that came unpleasantly athwart the border-line of scavenging. And from the trees that bounded and intersected the village rose the horrible, tireless, spiteful-sounding squawking of the iron-throated crows.

Comus sat and watched it all with a sense of growing aching depression. It was so utterly trivial to his eyes, so devoid of interest, and yet it was so real, so serious, so implacable in its continuity. The brain grew tired with the thought of its increasing reproduction. It had all gone on, as it was going on now, by the side of the great rushing, swirling river, this tilling and planting and harvesting, marketing and store-keeping, feast-making and fetish-worship and love-making, burying and giving in marriage, child-bearing and child-rearing, all this had been going on, in the shimmering, blistering heat and the warm nights, while he had been a youngster at school, dimly recognizing Africa as a division of the earth's surface that it was advisable to have a certain nodding acquaintance with. It had been going on in all its trifling detail, all its serious intensity, when his father and his grandfather in their day had been little boys at school, it would go on just as intently as ever long after Comus and his generation had passed away, just as the shadows would lengthen and fade under the mulberry trees in that far-away English garden, round the old stone fountain where a leaden otter for ever preyed on a leaden salmon.

Comus rose impatiently from his seat, and walked wearily across the hut to another window-opening which commanded a broad view of the river. There was something which fascinated and then depressed one in its ceaseless hurrying onward sweep, its tons of water rushing on for all time, as long as the face of the earth should remain unchanged. On its farther shore could be seen spread out at intervals other teeming villages, with their cultivated plots and pasture clearings, their moving dots which meant cattle and goats and dogs and children. And far up its course, lost in the forest growth that fringed its banks, were hidden away yet more villages, human herding-grounds where men dwelt and worked and bartered, squabbled and worshipped, sickened and perished while the river went by with its endless swirl and rush of gleaming waters. One could well understand primitive early races making propitiatory sacrifices to the spirit of a great river on whose shores they dwelt. Time and the river were the two great forces that seemed to matter here.

It was almost a relief to turn back to the other outlook and watch the village life that was now beginning to wake in earnest. The procession of water-fetchers had formed itself in a long chattering line that stretched riverwards. Comus wondered how many tens of thousands of times that procession had been formed since first the village came into existence. They had been doing it while he was playing in the cricket-fields at school, while he was spending Christmas holidays in Paris, while he was going his careless round of theatres, dances, suppers and card-parties, just as they were doing it now; they would be doing it when there was no one alive who remembered Comus Bassington. This thought recurred again and again with painful persistence, a morbid growth arising in part from his loneliness.

Staring dumbly out at the toiling, sweltering human ant-hill, Comus marvelled how missionary enthusiasts could labour hopefully at the work of transplanting their religion, with its home-grown accretions of fatherly parochial benevolence, in this heat-blistered, fever-scourged wilderness, where men lived like groundbait and died like flies. Demons one might believe in, if one did not hold one's imagination in healthy check, but a kindly all-managing God, never. Somewhere in the west country of England Comus had an uncle who lived in a rose-smothered rectory and taught a wholesome gentle-hearted creed that expressed itself in the spirit of 'Little lamb, Who made thee?' and faithfully reflected the beautiful homely Christ-child sentiment of Saxon Europe. What a far-away, unreal fairy-story it all seemed here in this West African land, where the bodies of men were of as little account as the bubbles that floated on the oily froth of the great flowing river, and where it required a stretch of wild profitless imagination to credit them with undying souls! In the life he had come from Comus had been accustomed to think of individuals as definite masterful personalities, making their several marks on the circumstances that revolved around them; they did well or ill, or in most cases indifferently, and were criticized, praised, blamed, thwarted, or tolerated, or given way to. In any case, humdrum or outstanding, they had their spheres of importance, little or big. They dominated a breakfast table or harassed a Government, according to their capabilities or opportunities, or perhaps they merely had irritating mannerisms. At any rate it seemed highly probable that they had souls. Here a man simply made a unit in an unnumbered population, an inconsequent dot in a loosely-compiled death-roll. Even his own position as a white man exalted conspicuously above a horde of black natives did not save Comus from the depressing sense of nothingness which his first experience of fever had thrown over him. He was a lost, soulless body in this great uncaring land; if he died another would take his place, his few effects would be inventoried and sent down to the coast, someone else would finish off any tea or whisky that he left behind—that would be all.

It was nearly time to be starting towards the next halting-place where he would dine, or at any rate eat something. But the lassitude which the fever had bequeathed him made the tedium of travelling through interminable forest-tracks a weariness to be deferred as long as possible. The bearers were nothing loath to let another half-hour or so slip by, and Comus dragged a battered paper-covered novel from the pocket of his coat. It was a story dealing with the elaborately tangled love affairs of a surpassingly uninteresting couple, and even in his almost bookless state Comus had not been able to plough his way through more than two-thirds of its dull length; bound up with the cover, however, were some pages of advertisement, and these the exile scanned with a hungry intentness that the romance itself could never have commanded. The name of a shop, of a street, the address of a restaurant, came to him as a bitter reminder of the world he had lost, a world that ate and drank and flirted, gambled and made merry, a world that debated and intrigued and wire-pulled, fought or compromised political battles—and recked nothing of its outcasts wandering through forest paths and steamy swamps or lying in the grip of fever. Comus read and re-read those few lines of advertisement, just as he treasured a much-crumpled programme of a first-night performance at the Straw Exchange Theatre; they seemed to make a little more real the past that was already so shadowy and so utterly remote. For a moment he could almost capture the sensation of being once again in those haunts that he loved; then he looked round and pushed the book wearily from him. The steaming heat, the forest, the rushing river hemmed him in on all sides.

The two boys who had been splitting wood ceased from their labours and straightened their backs; suddenly the smaller of the two gave the other a resounding whack with a split lath that he still held in his hand, and flew up the hillside with a scream of laughter and simulated terror, the bigger lad following in hot pursuit. Up and down the steep bush-grown slope they raced and twisted and dodged, coming sometimes to close quarters in a hurricane of squeals and smacks, rolling over and over like fighting kittens, and breaking away again to start fresh provocation and fresh pursuit. Now and again they would lie for a time panting in what seemed the last stage of exhaustion, and then they would be off in another wild scamper, their dusky bodies flitting through the bushes, disappearing and reappearing with equal suddenness. Presently two girls of their own age, who had returned from the water-fetching, sprang out on them from ambush, and the four joined in one joyous gambol that lit up the hillside with shrill echoes and glimpses of flying limbs. Comus sat and watched, at first with an amused interest, then with a returning flood of depression and heartache. Those wild young human kittens represented the joy of life, he was the outsider, the lonely alien, watching something in which he could not join, a happiness in which he had no part or lot. He would pass presently out of the village and his bearers' feet would leave their indentations in the dust: that would be his most permanent memorial in this little oasis of teeming life. And that other life, in which he once moved with such confident sense of his own necessary participation in it, how completely he had passed out of it! Amid all its laughing throngs, its card-parties and race-meetings and country-house gatherings, he was just a mere name, remembered or forgotten, Comus Bassington, the boy who went away. He had loved himself very well and never troubled greatly whether anyone else really loved him, and now he realized what he had made of his life. And at the same time he knew that if his chance were to come again he would throw it away just as surely, just as perversely. Fate played with him with loaded dice; he would lose always.

One person in the whole world had cared for him, for longer than he could remember, cared for him perhaps more than he knew, cared for him perhaps now. But a wall of ice had mounted up between him and her, and across it there blew that cold breath that chills or kills affection.

The words of a well-known old song, the wistful cry of a lost cause, rang with insistent mockery through his brain:

> *Better loved you canna be,*
> *Will ye ne'er come back again?*

If it was love that was to bring him back he must be an exile for ever. His epitaph in the mouths of those that remembered him would be: Comus Bassington, the boy who never came back.

And in his unutterable loneliness he bowed his head on his arms, that he might not see the joyous scrambling frolic on yonder hillside.

CHAPTER XVII

THE bleak rawness of a grey December day held sway over St James's Park, that sanctuary of lawn and tree and pool, into which the bourgeois innovator has rushed ambitiously time and again, to find that he must take the patent leather from off his feet, for the ground on which he stands is hallowed ground.

In the lonely hour of early afternoon, when the workers had gone back to their work, and the loiterers were scarcely yet gathered again, Francesca Bassington made her way restlessly along the stretches of gravelled walk that bordered the ornamental water. The overmastering unhappiness that filled her heart and stifled her thinking powers found answering echo in her surroundings. There is a sorrow that lingers in old parks and gardens that the busy streets have no leisure to keep by them; the dead must bury their dead in Whitehall or the Place de la Concorde, but there are quieter spots where they may still keep tryst with the living and intrude the memory of their bygone selves on generations that have almost forgotten them. Even in tourist-trampled Versailles the desolation of a tragedy that cannot die haunts the terraces and fountains like a blood-stain that will not wash out; in the Saxon Garden at Warsaw there broods the memory of long-dead things, coeval with the stately trees that shade its walks, and with the carp that swim to-day in its ponds as they doubtless swam there when 'Lieber Augustin' was a living person and not as yet an immortal couplet. And St James's Park, with its lawns and walks and water-fowl, harbours still its associations with a bygone order of men and women, whose happiness and sadness are woven into its history, dim and grey as they were once bright and glowing, like the faded pattern worked into the fabric of an old tapestry. It was here that Francesca had made her way when the intolerable inaction of waiting had driven her forth from her home. She was waiting for that worst news of all, the news which does not kill hope, because there has been none to kill, but merely ends suspense. An early message had said that Comus was ill, which might have meant much or little; then there had come that morning a cablegram which only meant one thing; in a few hours she would get a final message, of which this was the preparatory forerunner. She already knew as much as that awaited message would tell her. She knew that she would never see Comus again, and she knew now that she loved him beyond all things that the world could hold for her. It was no sudden rush of pity or compunction that clouded her judgment or gilded her recollection of him; she saw him as he was, the beautiful wayward laughing boy, with his naughtiness, his exasperating selfishness, his insurmountable folly and perverseness, his cruelty that spared not even himself, and as he was, as he always had been, she knew that he was the one thing that the Fates had willed that she should love. She did not stop to accuse or excuse herself for having sent him forth to what was to prove his death. It was, doubtless, right and reasonable that he should have gone out there, as hundreds of other men went out, in pursuit of careers; the terrible thing was that he would never come back. The old cruel hopelessness that had always chequered her pride and pleasure in his good looks and high spirits and fitfully charming ways had dealt her a crushing blow; he was dying somewhere thousands of miles away without hope of recovery, without a word of love to comfort him, and without hope or shred of consolation she was waiting to hear of the end. The end; that last dreadful piece of news which would write 'Nevermore' across his life and hers.

The lively bustle in the streets had been a torture that she could not bear. It wanted but two days to Christmas, and the gaiety of the season, forced or genuine, rang out everywhere. Christmas shopping, with its anxious solicitude or self-centred absorption, overspread the West End and made the pavements scarcely passable at certain favoured points. Proud parents, parcel-laden and surrounded by escorts of their young people, compared notes with one another on the looks and qualities of their offspring and exchanged loud hurried confidences on the difficulty or success which each had experienced in getting the right presents for one and all. Shouted directions where to find this or that article at its best mingled with salvos of Christmas good wishes. To Francesca, making her way frantically through the carnival of happiness with that lonely deathbed in her eyes, it had seemed a callous mockery of her pain; could not people remember that there were crucifixions as well as joyous birthdays in the world? Every mother that she passed happy in the company of a fresh-looking, clean-limbed schoolboy son sent a fresh stab at her heart, and the very shops had their bitter memories. There was the tea-shop where he and she had often taken tea together, or, in the days of their estrangement, sat with their separate friends at separate tables. There were other shops where extravagantly-incurred bills had furnished material for those frequently recurring scenes of recrimination, and the Colonial outfitters, where, as he had phrased it in whimsical mockery, he had bought grave-clothes for his burying-alive. The 'oubliette'! She remembered the bitter petulant name he had flung at his destined exile. There at least he had been harder on himself than the Fates were pleased to will; never, as long as Francesca lived and had a brain that served her, would she be able to forget. That narcotic would never be given to her. Unrelenting, unsparing memory would be with her always to remind her of those last days of tragedy. Already her mind was dwelling on the details of that ghastly farewell dinner-party and recalling one by one the incidents of ill-omen that had marked it; how they had sat down seven to table and how one liqueur glass in the set of seven had been shivered into fragments; how her glass had slipped from her hand as she raised it to her lips to wish Comus a safe return; and the strange, quiet hopelessness of Lady Veula's 'Good-bye'; she remembered now how it had chilled and frightened her at the moment.

The park was filling again with its floating population of loiterers, and Francesca's footsteps began to take a homeward direction. Something seemed to tell her that the message for which she waited had arrived and was lying there on the hall table. Her brother, who had announced his intention of visiting her early in the afternoon, would have gone by now; he knew nothing of this morning's bad news—the instinct of a wounded animal to creep away by itself had prompted her to keep her sorrow from him as long as possible. His visit did not necessitate her presence; he was bringing an Austrian friend, who was compiling a work on the Franco-Flemish school of painting, to inspect the Van der Meulen, which Henry Greech hoped might perhaps figure as an illustration in the book. They were due to arrive shortly after lunch, and Francesca had left a note of apology, pleading an urgent engagement elsewhere. As she turned to make her way across the Mall into the Green Park a gentle voice hailed her from a carriage that was just drawing up by the sidewalk. Lady Caroline Benaresq had been favouring the Victoria Memorial with a long unfriendly stare.

'In primitive days,' she remarked, 'I believe it was the fashion for great chiefs and rulers to have large numbers of their relatives and dependents killed and buried with them; in these more enlightened times we have invented quite another way of making a great sovereign universally regretted. My dear Francesca,' she broke off suddenly, catching the misery that had settled in the other's eyes, 'what is the matter? Have you had bad news from out there?'

'I am waiting for very bad news,' said Francesca, and Lady Caroline knew what had happened.

'I wish I could say something; I can't.' Lady Caroline spoke in a harsh, grunting voice that few people had ever heard her use.

Francesca crossed the Mall, and the carriage drove on.

'Heaven help that poor woman,' said Lady Caroline, which was, for her, startlingly like a prayer.

As Francesca entered the hall she gave a quick look at the table; several packages, evidently an early batch of Christmas presents, were there, and two or three letters. On a salver by itself was the cablegram for which she had waited. A maid, who had evidently been on the look-out for her, brought her the salver. The servants were well aware of the dreadful thing that was happening, and there was pity on the girl's face and in her voice.

'This came for you ten minutes ago, ma'am, and Mr Greech has been here, ma'am, with another gentleman, and was sorry you weren't at home. Mr Greech said he would call again in about half an hour.'

Francesca carried the cablegram unopened into the drawing-room and sat down for a moment to think. There was no need to read it yet, for she knew what she would find written there. For a few pitiful moments Comus would seem less hopelessly lost to her if she put off the reading of that last terrible message. She rose and crossed over to the windows and pulled down the blinds, shutting out the waning December day, and then re-seated herself. Perhaps in the shadowy half-light her boy would come and sit with her again for awhile and let her look her last upon his loved face; she could never touch him again or hear his laughing petulant voice, but surely she might look on her dead. And her starving eyes saw only the hateful soulless things of bronze and silver and porcelain that she had set up and worshipped as gods; look where she would they were there around her, the cold ruling deities of the home that held no place for her dead boy. He had moved in and out among them, the warm, living, breathing thing that had been hers to love, and she had turned her eyes from that youthful comely figure to adore a few feet of painted canvas, a musty relic of a long departed craftsman. And now he was gone from her sight, from her touch, from her hearing for ever, without even a thought to flash between them for all the dreary years that she should live, and these things of canvas and pigment and wrought metal would stay with her. They were her soul. And what shall it profit a man if he save his soul and slay his heart in torment?

On a small table by her side was Mervyn Quentock's portrait of her—the prophetic symbol of her tragedy; the rich dead harvest of unreal things that had never known life, and the bleak thrall of black unending Winter, a Winter in which things died and knew no re-awakening.

Francesca turned to the small envelope lying in her lap; very slowly she opened it and read the short message. Then she sat numb and silent for a long, long time, or perhaps only for minutes. The voice of Henry Greech in the hall, inquiring for her, called her to herself. Hurriedly she crushed the piece of paper out of sight; he would have to be told, of course, but just yet her pain seemed too dreadful to be laid bare. 'Comus is dead' was a sentence beyond her power to speak.

'I have bad news for you, Francesca, I'm sorry to say,' Henry announced. Had he heard, too?

'Henneberg has been here and looked at the picture,' he continued, seating himself by her side, 'and though he admired it immensely as a work of art, he gave me a disagreeable surprise by assuring me that it's not a genuine Van der Meulen. It's a splendid copy, but still, unfortunately, only a copy.'

Henry paused and glanced at his sister to see how she had taken the unwelcome announcement. Even in the dim light he caught some of the anguish in her eyes.

'My dear Francesca,' he said soothingly, laying his hand affectionately on her arm, 'I know that this must be a great disappointment to you, you've always set such store by this picture, but you mustn't take it too much to heart. These disagreeable discoveries come at times to most picture fanciers and owners. Why, about twenty per cent of the alleged Old Masters in the Louvre are supposed to be wrongly attributed. And there are heaps of similar cases in this country. Lady Dovecourt was telling me the other day that they simply daren't have an expert in to examine the Van Dykes at Columbey for fear of unwelcome disclosures. And, besides, your picture is such an excellent copy that it's by no means without a value of its own. You must get over the disappointment you naturally feel, and take a philosophical view of the matter. . . .'

Francesca sat in stricken silence, crushing the folded morsel of paper tightly in her hand and wondering if the thin, cheerful voice with its pitiless, ghastly mockery of consolation would never stop.